WHISPERS BEYOND THE RAILS

One Voice. One Secret. One Chance to Be Heard

Author

Sumit Sharma MBA, FHFMA, SCPM, SSMBB

Copyright and Legal Notice

Important Disclaimer

Whispers Beyond the Rails is intended to be a creative and inspirational work for teens and young adults. While the

Foreword

As a psychologist who has spent decades working with adolescents navigating the complex intersections of identity, belonging, and mental health, I found Whispers Beyond the Rails to be both haunting and healing. This is not just

a novel—it is a mirror held up to the silent battles fought daily in high school hallways, classrooms, and lunchrooms across the country. Sumit Sharma's writing is bold in its emotional honesty and nuanced in its portrayal of youth trauma, bias, and the quiet resilience of teenagers. Through characters like Evan, Kiera, and Tyler, the book offers a deeply moving look at what it means to be unheard—and what it takes to truly listen. This book does more than tell a story. It opens a door for dialogue. It challenges students, parents, teachers, and mental health professionals alike to examine the culture of silence that surrounds us and to ask: What whispers have we ignored? And what might change if we finally paid attention?

I believe Whispers Beyond the Rails will not only resonate with young readers but serve as a resource for schools hoping to build emotionally safe and inclusive environments. I am honored to introduce this book and hope it finds its way into many classrooms, homes, and hearts.

J.R. Evans Psy. D.

Banner University Medical Center Phoenix, AZ

About the Author

Sumit Sharma

Sumit Sharma is a dedicated mentor, author, and leadership coach, passionate about empowering young minds. He is the author of ***Em-powering Tomorrow's Leaders: A Guide for Teens***, a practical and inspiring resource designed to help teenagers develop confidence, communication skills, and leadership abilities.

With over 20 years of experience in leadership, strategy, and coaching, Sumit has spent countless hours guiding teenagers toward discovering their voice, building resilience, and overcoming obstacles. His pro bono work with youth programs, including teaching design thinking to high school students, reflects his deep commitment to empowering future leaders.

Sumit blends his dedication to mental well-being, youth empowerment, and community resilience in ***Whispers Beyond the Rails***. Through this powerful narrative, he aims to inspire young readers to recognize their voices' strength and their profound impact on the world.

In a narrative format, Sumit details a training module targeted at adolescents and young adults, creating safe spaces where voices will be heard. Starting out slow, he describes how to implement his ideas in schools, then expand into the community at large, and ultimately, globally. These strategies enable those afraid, to speak up, be heard, and realize others do care.

Sumit lives with his family in Arizona, where he continues to mentor, write, and inspire positive change.

The WHISPER Model™

A Framework for Connection, Compassion, and Courage

The WHISPER Model™ is a structured, actionable framework designed to help individuals create safe spaces, foster meaningful connections, and provide compassionate support to those in need. Inspired by *Whispers of the Third Rail*, this model reflects the power of quiet actions and small moments of kindness that ripple outward to change lives.

The WHISPER Model™ is an acronym that stands for:

W — Watch for Silent Signals

H — Hold Space Without Judgment

I — Initiate a Safe Conversation

S — Speak with Empathy

P — Practice Active Support

E — Encourage Professional Help

R — Reinforce Resilience and Hope

TABLE OF CONTENTS

Dedication

To my parents, Mr. V. N. Sharma, I.P.S., and Prof. Dr. Meena Sharma, for teaching me the power of compassion, resilience, and standing firm in the face of adversity.

To my wife, Deepti Sharma, for being my anchor, partner, and constant source of strength and encouragement.

To my children, Savar, Saesha, and Vyom, for reminding me that we leave the most significant impact through the love, lessons, and values we pass down.

To my brother, Varun Sharma, and my sister, Dr. Bulbul Salwan, for their steadfast support and belief in me.

And finally, to every young adult who has ever felt unheard — may you find the courage to speak, the strength to stand, and the wisdom to realize your voice matters.

❖ To those who suffer in silence — may you know that your voice matters.

❖ To the quiet observers — your courage can change everything.

❖ And to those brave enough to listen — you are the heartbeat of hope.

May this book remind us that even the faintest whisper can spark change.

Prologue

The whisper came before the silence.

It started as nothing more than a murmur — a rumor shared in hurried conversations, scrawled on the margins of notebooks, and whispered between friends when no one else was listening. Most people ignored it, brushing it off as just another teenage rumor — the kind floating through River Valley High every week. But those who paid attention knew better. The whisper wasn't gossip. It wasn't noise.

It was a warning.

Tyler had walked the halls of River Valley like a shadow — never entirely fitting in, never quite seen. His quietness made him easy to overlook. He wasn't a troublemaker. He wasn't a star athlete. He wasn't popular or infamous — just there, quietly drawing in his sketchbook or disappearing into the corners of the library. And then, one day, Tyler wasn't there. At all.

No one knew what to say. The morning after his death, the

school buzzed with speculation — guesses, half-truths, and careless theories disguised as facts.

"He was dealing with stuff," someone whispered near the lockers. "His family... things weren't good at home," another voice added. But no one knew.

By lunchtime, a new post appeared on RiverChat, the school's anonymous social platform — a platform students used to vent, gossip, and share news without revealing their identities. This post was different. It was short, sharp, and cold:

You're all pretending you cared. But you didn't. Not really. He tried to speak once. You didn't listen.

The post was signed by someone calling themselves The Third Rail.

River Valley students knew the name. The Third Rail posted cryptic messages hinting at things no one wanted to discuss. But this post struck harder than anything prior. It wasn't just words. It felt personal — like a punch to the chest.

Evan read the post three times before closing his phone. The words clung to him like smoke, curling into every corner of his mind.

He tried to speak once... You didn't listen.

He thought about Tyler sitting alone at lunch, Tyler staying late in the art room, Tyler walking the hallways like a shadow.

And then Evan thought about that moment — the one he had pushed from his mind.

The day Tyler stood near his locker, eyes red and tired. He had tried to say something — Evan was sure of it now — but Evan had been too distracted to listen. He'd mumbled a rushed goodbye and hurried off, thinking whatever Tyler wanted to say could wait.

But now Tyler was gone. And whatever he had tried to say was gone with him.

You didn't listen.

The words returned, louder now.

That night, Evan couldn't sleep. He kept seeing Tyler's face, hearing his voice, remembering that moment when he could have stopped — when he should have stopped — but didn't. He wondered who The Third Rail was and how they knew.

But what haunted Evan most was the fear that whoever they were... They were right.

Chapter 1: The Whisper That Started It All

Whispers

The whispers started the morning after Tyler's death. At first, soft murmurs circulated throughout the school — rumors exchanged in hushed tones behind locker doors and scribbled on scraps of notebook paper. By lunchtime, however, it seemed everyone at River Valley High had a theory. Some claimed Tyler hid a secret. Others insisted his last moments were filled with desperate arguments and silent pleas. Yet, amid all the speculation, no one truly understood the depth of his silence.

Kiera sat in the back of the cafeteria; her eyes fixed on her tray as the noise around her blurred into an indistinct hum. The steady throb of her thoughts drowned out the cacophony of conversations and clattering dishes — her thoughts continually circled back to Tyler.

How had she missed it? He had always been quiet, blending effortlessly into the background. Whether lost in the pages of his worn art pad or strumming his guitar quietly behind the gym, Tyler's subtle signals went unnoticed. Perhaps someone saw them, but no one ever asked the right questions.

"It's like he was invisible," muttered Evan from across the table. His voice, rough, as if he hadn't slept in days, carried an edge of remorse. "Like he was drowning, and none of us noticed."

Kiera's heart ached as she met his gaze. The regret in Evan's eyes mirrored the guilt churning within her. She had been preoccupied with leading student council meetings, organizing events, and trying to keep the chaos of River Valley High in check. In her pursuit of epitomizing the strong leader everyone depended on, she failed to see the silent suffering of a friend.

After the cafeteria's clamor faded into the sounds of hallways emptying between classes, Kiera slipped into a deserted classroom. Light slanted in through dusty windows, casting long shadows on the walls. Here, in the quiet, she let her thoughts spill out.

I was so busy being in control, always on top of everything... But what about Tyler? Blinded by my responsibilities, I never saw his silent cries for help. Did I miss his pain because it was easier to pretend everything was normal?

Her mind replayed snippets from memory — the brief moments when Tyler's eyes spoke volumes, his shoulders slumped a little lower than usual, and he tucked a small note into his notebook that read, *I wish someone would notice*. In the stillness, Kiera realized her own perfectionism and sense of duty came at a steep price. She had been too distracted to see the quiet storm of Tyler's loneliness raging below the surface.

That evening, as dusk settled and the campus fell into a somber silence, a new post appeared on RiverChat. No one knew who ran the Third Rail account, but its messages gained notoriety for stirring controversy and unearthing buried truths. Some speculated the account belonged to a teacher disillusioned with the system, while others believed it was the bitter outburst of a senior with too much time on their hands. Still, the truth remained elusive. This post, however, felt different; it carried an urgency striking a deep, personal chord.

He walked these halls like a ghost. You never saw him unless you looked

— but no one ever did. Now he's gone, and you're all pretending you cared. But you didn't. Not really.

Kiera's hands trembled as she reread the message. It hit her like a punch to the chest. Whispers quickly spread among the students that The Third Rail knew something no one else did — maybe Tyler's death was not as simple as it seemed.

Later that night, as Kiera sat alone in her room under the dim glow of a bedside lamp, her phone buzzed with a call from Evan. His voice, heavy with regret, broke the silence.

"Maybe they're right," he said. "Maybe we didn't care enough."

Kiera's heart pounded as she whispered, "We did... I did." But even as she tried to convince herself, doubt gnawed at her — had she seen him, heard him?

The day after the announcement of Tyler's death shrouded the hallways of River Valley High in a tangible heaviness. Every step taken by students seemed to echo with unspoken grief. A subdued murmur replaced the familiar clamor of lockers slamming and casual chatter, as if the entire school collectively held its breath. In these long, quiet corridors, students felt Tyler's absence in every corner — both physically and emotionally.

Kiera strolled the hall, her footsteps deliberate yet burdened. Each stride carried with it a weight of regret and introspection. She remembered the days when Tyler would slip quietly away from the crowd, finding solace in the art room where he sketched abstract figures and swirling landscapes — a language of his own making. Now, every empty seat and every silent locker spoke of his loss.

She found herself drawn to Tyler's old locker. A photo of him — from his freshman year when his hair was longer and his smile more open — was affixed to the door. The image radiated warmth and hope, a stark contrast to the cold indifference he had often faced. The image contrasted sharply with the cruel whispers in the hall.

"No wonder he always kept to himself," one student murmured. Another added, "He probably thought he'd embarrass his family."

Turning, Kiera saw Ben Mitchell, a junior infamous for his biting remarks.

"What's that supposed to mean?" Kiera asked sharply.

Ben shrugged, his tone dismissive. "I'm just saying... he was different. I didn't really... you know." His voice trailed off, leaving the implication hanging in the air.

Kiera's eyes narrowed as she considered his words. Everyone treated Tyler like an outsider — quiet, artistic, with a family failing to match the polished image of most River Valley students. His father worked as a mechanic, and his mother cleaned houses — a fact that, though rarely discussed openly, had not escaped the judgment of some peers. Kiera recalled overhearing snide remarks in sophomore year: "Tyler isn't River Valley material," they'd whispered. Kiera now realized the subtle bias and the unspoken judgment left Tyler feeling more diminutive and isolated daily.

Later that afternoon, as Kiera navigated the crowded hallway, she overheard a group of students near Tyler's locker.

"Did you know his mom used to clean Mrs. Hargrove's house?" one girl whispered. "No wonder he always kept to himself."

Another voice joined in, "He probably felt embarrassed. People like that don't fit in here."

Kiera clenched her fists, her heart pounding with anger and sorrow. Tyler should never have felt inferior because of his family background. She remembered the many afternoons when Tyler lingered in the art room long after the rest of the class had left, with his head bowed over his sketchbook, as if searching for solace. Her chest ached with regret.

As darkness enveloped the school that evening, Evan texted Kiera a screenshot of another Third Rail post. This one felt even more haunting:

He tried to speak once. He tried to tell someone what he was carrying. But some people don't want to hear what doesn't fit their perfect picture. So, they turned away.

The message reverberated in Kiera's mind.

"Do you think it's true?" Kiera asked Evan the following day, her voice laced with dread, after contemplating the words throughout the night.

"I don't know," he replied softly, "but I think...I think I know what Tyler was trying to say." He hesitated, then added, "There was this one time... after the gym... Tyler told me he felt like he didn't belong here. Said people looked at him like he was... wrong."

"Why didn't you say anything before?" Shock and regret mingled in Kiera's tone.

"Because I didn't think it mattered." Evan's voice cracked with guilt. "I thought he was just venting. I told him to forget about it." He swallowed hard. "But what if... what if he needed someone to tell him he did belong?"

Kiera felt her chest tighten as she considered his words. Tyler had spent so much time surrounded by whispers about his family, clothes, and quiet nature. Perhaps he internalized those hurtful messages, believing they were true. Maybe he thought that was all he'd ever be.

The weight of Evan's confession clung to the air as they walked silently down the hallway later that morning. A small group of students gathered around Tyler's locker, quietly placing flowers and handwritten notes. The whispers continued — but carried a different tone. Quieter and softer. As if each note held a silent plea to rectify the neglect. It was as if everyone knew, deep down, something crucial had been missed — a chance to save a life.

Kiera's Inner Battle: The Weight of Responsibility

After the bell rang and students filed into their classes, Kiera stole away to an empty classroom. Sitting at a creaking wooden desk, she pulled out her journal and let her thoughts spill onto the paper. She wrote about the pressure of leadership, the endless meetings, and the constant drive to keep everything together. But now, Tyler's memory haunted her.

I was so caught up in being strong, in leading everyone, that I failed to see a friend who was silently breaking. I thought his silence was typical — just the way he was. But maybe it wasn't normal at all. Perhaps it was a desperate cry for help that I chose to ignore because it was easier than facing my shortcomings.

Her eyes stung with tears as she recalled the countless times she had passed by Tyler without genuinely seeing him. In her mind's eye, she saw him sitting alone in the art room, his eyes fixed on a blank page, waiting for someone to notice. That image seared into her memory. No one should feel invisible.

A Glimpse into Tyler's World: The Homefront and the Bias

That same evening, Kiera's thoughts wandered to what little she knew about Tyler's life outside of school. She recalled overhearing fragments of conversation about his family. Tyler's father, a hardworking mechanic, spent long hours in a noisy, oil-stained garage, while his mother, gentle and resilient, cleaned houses in an affluent neighborhood.

Tyler never spoke of his home life in detail, but the whispers revealed a painful truth: his family's background set him apart in a school that prized conformity and polish. She remembered a conversation during sophomore year when students remarked dismissively, "Tyler isn't River Valley material. His folks aren't like ours."

These words, spoken without malice but with prejudice, demolished Tyler's self-esteem. He began believing his self-worth was tied to his origin. Kiera's heart ached as she envisioned Tyler sitting alone in a darkened room after school, trying to hide the sting of those words behind his sketches and muted smile.

Kiera clenched her fists, the injustice of it all burning inside her. Tyler had never chosen his background, yet it had defined him in the eyes of many.

The Third Rail's Haunting Echoes

As dusk settled and the campus grew silent, Kiera's phone buzzed with another message from The Third Rail. This time, the post was even more desperate, more anguished:

I tried to scream, but the silence was all that met my cry. Now I'm just another ghost in these halls, forgotten by those who promised to see me.

Kiera stared at the screen, the words echoing in her mind. Tyler's voice, a final, desperate outcry, lost in daily life's noise. She felt the weight of every neglected moment, every ignored sign of distress. A reminder of the day Tyler told Evan, after gym, that he felt like he didn't belong — a picture now burned into her psyche.

The following day, as she walked with Evan in the corridor, she struggled to reconcile the boy she thought she knew with the painful truth revealed by these posts.

"Do you think we could have done something differently?" Kiera asked in a hushed tone.

Evan's eyes were downcast. "I don't know... I wish I'd listened more. I wish I'd seen what he tried to tell us."

Kiera's heart ached at his words. In that shared moment of regret, they both understood that Tyler's silence had been a call for help — a call they had tragically missed.

A Confrontation with Bias: Facing Ben

In the days following the unsettling Third Rail posts, the atmosphere at River Valley High became even more charged with unspoken emotions and simmering tensions. Discussions began quietly among small groups, gradually escalated into debates over the true nature of belonging and acceptance. In this climate, Kiera knew a confrontation with Ben Mitchell was inevitable — a confrontation she both dreaded and realized was necessary for healing.

One crisp afternoon, as the final bell rang and students hurried out of class in huddled groups, Kiera found herself alone in a quiet corridor near the art room. The fading light cast long shadows along the lockers, creating an almost surreal backdrop for what she was about to do. Her heart pounded as she approached Ben, standing near Tyler's old locker with a few other seniors.

Ben's eyes were fixed on the same locker where delicate flowers and handwritten notes had been placed in memory of Tyler. His expression was impassive, yet there was a subtle arrogance in how he held himself — a quiet reminder of the unchallenged biases that plagued the school.

Taking a deep breath, Kiera stepped forward. "Ben," she called, her voice echoing softly down the hallway.

Ben turned, his gaze meeting hers with curiosity and defensiveness. "Yeah?" he replied, his tone neutral.

Kiera's eyes hardened. "I need to know — what did you mean when you said Tyler was 'different' and that he didn't belong?"

For a moment, silence hung between them. Ben's confident façade wavered as he shifted his weight. "I — I just meant that Tyler wasn't like the rest of us," he stammered. "You know, his background... his family."

Kiera's face flushed with a mix of anger and sorrow. "Different? You mean because his dad is a mechanic and his mom cleans houses?" Her voice rose, each word measured and deliberate. "Do you believe that defines who he is?"

Ben hesitated, his eyes flickering with uncertainty. "It's not about defining him," he murmured, his voice lowering as if to hide behind the walls of his discomfort. "It's just... people have expectations, Kiera. Tyler didn't quite match that ideal in a school like this, where everyone is expected to fit a certain image. It's nothing personal."

"Nothing personal?" Kiera repeated, her tone icy. "But it was personal to him! And it's personal to everyone who cares enough to see him for who he was. Your words made him feel like he wasn't enough — like he was less than, simply because he didn't come from a family that fits your narrow view of what belongs here."

Ben's eyes darted away, and the corridor seemed to hold its breath for a long moment. "I... I never thought about it like that," he finally said, his voice barely a whisper. "I always assumed it was just a harmless observation — just a fact."

Kiera's expression softened, though her resolve remained firm. "A fact? Ben, those 'facts' have consequences. They create an environment where people like Tyler feel isolated and unworthy. When you say someone doesn't belong because of their background, you're not just stating an observation — you're reinforcing a system of bias that tells people they're invisible."

A murmur of discontent rippled among the nearby students. Ben's posture stiffened as he struggled to maintain his composure. "Look, I didn't mean to hurt anyone," he said defensively. "I didn't think it would be taken so personally."

Kiera stepped even closer, her eyes locked on his. "Did you think Tyler would simply fade away because of that? Did you think that his quiet nature was acceptable because it fit your ideal of who should belong? I'm telling you, Ben, every word we speak, every remark we make, shapes how someone sees themselves. Tyler's silence wasn't a choice — it was a result of feeling rejected, of hearing those biased whispers every day."

Ben's face contorted with a mixture of anger and regret. "Maybe...I don't know," he said slowly. "I guess I never really considered how much those words might hurt."

Kiera's voice softened slightly, though her eyes burned with determination. "It's not just about hurting him, Ben. It's about the message it sends to everyone else who feels different and comes from a background that isn't celebrated here. If we allow these biases to go unchallenged, then every quiet soul will learn that their worth is measured by where they come from, not who they are."

A heavy silence fell over them, punctuated only by the distant hum of a nearby class. In that moment, Kiera saw something in Ben's eyes — a flicker of understanding, perhaps even remorse. "I'm sorry," he finally mumbled, his voice fragile. "I didn't mean... I never wanted to hurt him."

"An apology is a start," Kiera replied, her tone gentler now. "But you need to understand that words have power. They can either lift someone or push them further into darkness. Tyler needed us to see him — not just as a statistic or a quiet boy who didn't fit in, but as a person with dreams, feelings, and a right to belong."

As the corridor filled with the murmurs of other students, Ben looked at the wall where Tyler's locker stood, adorned with flowers and notes. "I see it now," he said quietly, almost to himself. "I do. And I'm sorry I never looked deeper."

Kiera nodded, feeling a small measure of relief. "We all have our blind spots, Ben. The important thing is that we learn from them and work to ensure no one else is made to feel less than or that they don't belong."

After their exchange, the tension in the hallway seemed to ease slightly, replaced by a cautious understanding. Having overheard parts of the conversation, other students began approaching Tyler's locker. They added fresh flowers and new notes — messages not of judgment but of hope and solidarity. Hastily written in red ink, one note read: *We see you. You matter.*

Ben lingered near the locker, his eyes glued to the note as if trying to absorb its meaning. In that quiet moment, he realized the part he played in the biased culture within River Valley High. And now he understood the impact.

Kiera watched as Ben, Evan, and a few other students quietly gathered around, discussing how they might start conversations that mattered — conversations that challenged the status quo and embraced every voice, no matter how soft. The corridor, once filled with the echoes of whispered biases, was slowly turning into a space of open dialogue and tentative understanding.

With a deep, steadying breath, Kiera stepped back, allowing the scene to unfold. In her heart, she knew this confrontation was just one step in a long journey toward change. But it was a vital step — a declaration that the legacy of Tyler would be one of compassion, awareness, and, above all, the courage to speak out against the biases that robbed him of a chance to be seen.

Building the Atmosphere: A School in Transition

As twilight fell over River Valley High, the hallways took on a somber, almost sacred quality that evening. Lined with lockers and fading posters, the once-familiar corridors seemed to hold their breath. In one long, echoing hallway, a single beam of light from a narrow window illuminated a row of lockers, creating a stark contrast between shadow and brightness. It was a visual metaphor for Tyler's isolation — where even the light struggled to reach him.

Final Reflections: The Whisper That Endures

In the quiet moments after the day's tumult subsided, Kiera found herself alone near the now-familiar locker. The soft glow of dusk bathed the corridor in gentle light, and the whispered echoes of the day mingled with the silent promise of tomorrow. She pulled out her journal and wrote a single line that encapsulated everything she felt:

In every quiet moment, in every whispered memory, Tyler lives on — reminding us to see the unseen, to hear the unheard, and never to let anyone drown in silence.

She closed the journal and allowed herself a deep, shuddering breath. The journey ahead was uncertain, and the scars of loss would never fully fade. But with every step and act of kindness, Tyler's legacy would become a beacon — a whisper that, when joined by many, would grow into a resounding roar of hope.

Chapter 2: Unanswered Questions

The Heavy Aftermath

Images of Tyler's gentle smile and downcast eyes resurfaced with painful clarity in her mind. Melanie recalled those fleeting moments when his face would betray a hidden sorrow, moments that now seemed like desperate, silent pleas for help. *How could we have missed it?* She wondered repeatedly, the question echoing in her heart, as she sketched a memory of Tyler, bent over his art pad, across from her in class.

Across the corridor, Evan sat at a lone desk near a window. The soft, golden light of the morning filtered through, casting long shadows that danced slowly on the worn wooden floor. His fingers tapped restlessly on his notebook, a muted beat of his mounting remorse. Evan's eyes were distant, lost in memories of Tyler — a friend whose soft voice once tried to break through the noise, only to be drowned out by the relentless rush of everyday life.

During homeroom, while most students attempted to settle into the rhythm of the day, Kiera found herself staring out of a classroom window. The view was bittersweet: the campus bathed in a gentle, melancholy glow, yet beneath the beauty lay the raw pain of loss. She could almost hear Tyler's quiet sighs carried by the breeze — a reminder of the isolation he endured even in moments when the world around him seemed to flourish.

Whispers of speculation ran through the hallways as the day wore on. In hushed voices, students debated theories about what happened, as if speaking of it, they might somehow piece together the mystery of Tyler's final days. But for those who had known him even in passing, it was clear that Tyler's quiet demeanor was not a sign of indifference — it was a veil over the pain he carried, an invisible barrier that prevented him from asking for help.

A group of students gathered in one of the quieter corridors near the art room. Fresh flowers, carefully chosen and placed with trembling hands, were laid gently against the cold, unyielding metal of his locker. Handwritten notes, some written in a neat, cursive script and others hastily scrawled, adorned the makeshift memorial.

One note, yellowed at the edges and barely legible, read: *I wish someone would have seen me.* The simple words resonated deeply with Kiera as she read them; a stark, painful reminder of how Tyler slipped through the cracks of their attention.

At that moment, a teacher passed by — a quiet, thoughtful woman known for her gentle manner. She paused by the group, offering a brief, knowing look before continuing. Her silent acknowledgment felt like a small beacon, affirming they were not the only ones who felt the weight of his loss.

For Kiera, the sight was a trigger — a call to awaken from the numbing routine of leadership that left her oblivious to the quieter cries of those around her. As she stood there, the noise of the school seemed to fade into the background, replaced by a chorus of regrets. Every whispered comment, every silent judgment that had been passed about Tyler's quiet nature now coalesced into a single, resounding truth: they all failed to truly see him.

Evan's phone buzzed, shattering the fragile silence. Kiera glanced at it, and her heart sank as she saw a new message from The Third Rail on RiverChat. With a hesitant hand, Evan read the post aloud:

I tried to speak, but silence answered me. Now, the echo of my voice is lost in the void.

The words reverberated in the quiet of the corridor, each syllable a reminder of unheeded cries and lost opportunities. Kiera felt her throat tighten. The post was not merely a lament but a warning, an indictment of the pervasive indifference that allowed Tyler's pain to go unnoticed. At that moment, the gravity of their collective failure pressed down on her with an almost physical force.

As the school day wore on, Kiera and Evan were drawn together by this shared burden of regret. They walked side by side through the hallways, their silence speaking volumes more than words could. Every exchanged glance recognized an unspoken agreement that something had to change — that silence alone could not define Tyler's legacy.

Outside, the world continued as usual — a muted dance of shadows and light — but within the walls of River Valley High, the absence of Tyler transformed every whispered conversation into a prayer for redemption. The atmosphere, thick with regret as if every student waited for someone to break the cycle of silence and finally make sense of the unanswered questions.

The Spark of Regret

After the heavy silence that followed the day's first reflections, the school's corridors began to pulse with the quiet stirrings of regret. During the break between classes, as morning light faded into a tired afternoon, Evan was alone in a nearly empty corridor. The hum of distant chatter was subdued as if the entire school were mourning. In that quiet, he allowed himself to replay the realization from the previous day — the one where Tyler's muted confession had finally broken through his defenses.

Evan stopped near a row of lockers, his hand grazing the cool metal of Tyler's locker as if he could feel the ghost of his friend lingering there. He closed his eyes, summoning the memory of Tyler's soft voice, barely above a whisper: "I feel like I don't belong here." The words echoed through him, stirring a deep sense of regret. How often had he brushed off that plea as another fleeting moment?

How frequently had he ignored the subtle signs — the downcast eyes, the hesitant smile — that Tyler was suffering?

Evan's mind drifted back to an afternoon from a few weeks ago. He remembered sitting with Tyler under the bleachers after gym class when the school noise seemed to fade away. Tyler had leaned his head on his hand, eyes fixed on the distant horizon, and in that silence, Evan thought he saw a profound sadness. But he had been too caught up in his own distractions, too scared to ask, "What's wrong?" Now, that memory burned, an ember in his chest — a spark of regret threatening to ignite into something more.

Evan's thoughts were interrupted by the sound of footsteps echoing down the hall. Slowly, as if each step was measured in sorrow, a few more students joined him. Among them was a quiet boy with glasses, whose eyes betrayed a deep internal struggle, and a girl clutched a stack of notebooks with doodles in the margins. They didn't speak; they simply stood there, their silence, a mutual understanding of a loss too profound for words.

Meanwhile, Kiera stood at her locker, her mind whirling with conflicting emotions. The weight of Tyler's memory pressed on her, and she began to question every moment she had spent too busy to notice a friend in pain. *Could I have done something differently?* she wondered silently. Her thoughts drifted back to an instance during a student council meeting when she had dismissed Tyler's fleeting comment about feeling out of place. She remembered his eyes, the slight furrow of his brow — small gestures now carrying immense significance.

Determined to confront her regrets, Kiera pulled out her phone and scrolled through old messages between her and Tyler. One particular message caught her eye — a brief, almost casual note he sent during a quiet afternoon in the library: *Sometimes I feel like I'm shouting inside, but no one hears me.* The simple, vulnerable admission made her stomach twist with guilt. In that moment, Kiera resolved she would no longer let lonely voices feel unwelcome. She needed to find a way to honor Tyler's memory, to ensure no whisper of pain would be ignored again.

Later that day, as the school's routine continued, the tension began to build gradually. Evan and Kiera met in a quiet corner of the library during a free period. Surrounded by rows of dusty books and dim lights, they discussed the heavy burden they both felt.

"I can't stop thinking about what I should have done," Evan confessed, his voice barely audible over the soft rustle of pages. "Every time I remember Tyler telling me how out of place he felt, it's like a needle in my heart."

Kiera reached out and gently squeezed his hand. "I feel it, too. Every moment we ignored his silent cries, he built up this overwhelming isolation. But maybe we can do something now. We have to, for him."

They sat together silently for a long while, each lost in thought. The library's quiet was punctuated only by the sound of rain beginning to tap against the windows outside — a gentle, persistent rhythm mirroring their inner turmoil.

As the rain increased, Evan's phone buzzed again. Another message from The Third Rail flashed on the screen:

I tried to scream, but only echoes answered. Drowning in the void, I became nothing more than a ghost.

This time, the message felt even more urgent   a desperate cry from someone who felt utterly abandoned. Evan showed the message to Kiera, and together, they stared at it silently. The raw emotion in those words was unmistakable. They knew too well that such silent pleas were not rare; they were the norm for those who felt invisible.

Evan leaned forward, his eyes intense with remorse. "Kiera, I wish I'd understood sooner. I wish I'd been braver or maybe more aware. Every day, I wonder if one small act of compassion could have changed everything."

Kiera nodded, her own eyes brimming with tears. "We can't change what's already happened," she said softly. "But we can learn from it. We have to ensure no one else feels as alone as Tyler."

The Third Rail's Haunting Echoes

As the days wore on after the first shocking post, the whispers from The Third Rail became a constant, haunting presence. Every time a new message appeared on RiverChat, it sent ripples through the entire school. It wasn't long before these cryptic messages evolved from mere laments into urgent calls for attention.

One crisp, gray afternoon, when the corridors were empty, and the sound of rain against the windows filled the silence, Evan sat alone in a dimly lit classroom. He stared at his phone, his mind still reeling from the earlier posts. The screen suddenly lit up again — a new message from The Third Rail.

I tried to scream, but only echoes answered. My pleas dissolved into nothingness, leaving a void where hope once lived.

Evan's heart pounded as he read the words. This message was different — darker, more desperate. It wasn't just about being ignored anymore; it felt like a final, anguished cry. He couldn't shake the image of Tyler's silent eyes, full of unspoken pain and the feeling that he had been left to drown in a sea of indifference.

Unable to contain his turmoil, Evan called Kiera immediately. "Kiera, have you seen this?" he said, his voice trembling. "It's like the words are coming straight from his soul. I'm scared — they sound like a warning."

Kiera's response was soft but resolute. "I'm on my way," she replied. As she hurried through the halls, her mind raced. She recalled an earlier post that struck her hard, and now, this one made it clear the pain was escalating. It was as if each new message peeled back another layer of a hidden sorrow — a sorrow festering in silence.

They met in a quiet corner of the library, far from prying eyes. Evan held his phone tightly, showing Kiera the message once more. For several long moments, neither spoke. The words etched themselves into the space between them, heavy with meaning and foreboding.

Kiera finally broke the silence. "Do you think it could be Tyler's voice? Even after he's gone?" she whispered, her eyes searching Evan's face for answers.

Evan hesitated before replying, "I don't know, but it feels like he's trying to reach out from beyond the silence — a desperate attempt to make us understand his pain wasn't just his own." He ran a hand through his hair as if trying to smooth out the tangles of regret and sorrow accumulating inside him.

Over the next few days, the posts from The Third Rail became more frequent and more cryptic. One evening, as the school settled into a somber silence, another message flashed on Evan's screen:

When you ignore the whispers, they grow into screams no one hears. I am the ghost of unspoken truths.

This time, Evan felt a chill that went beyond regret. It was as if the post was a call to arms — a warning that the cycle of neglect and indifference could escalate into something far more dangerous if they ignored the suffering around them.

Kiera spent that night restless, tossing and turning as she tried deciphering the hidden meanings behind each post. She scribbled frantic notes in her journal in the quiet hours before dawn. *What if these messages are not just echoes of Tyler's pain but signals of a more profound, systemic failure?* she wondered. *Are we witnessing a warning of what happens when we ignore those who need us most?*

The following day, the atmosphere in the hallways was noticeably different. Whispers about Tyler and the cryptic posts seemed to have ignited something within the student body. Groups huddled in corners, discussing the posts in hushed, urgent tones. Even teachers appeared more attentive, their eyes lingering on Tyler's locker as if in silent apology.

Evan and Kiera sat near the window during lunch, the gray light of a wintry day filtering through. "I talked to a few students," Kiera said quietly. "Some admitted that they always felt like they were just... background noise. Like their voices didn't matter." Her voice broke slightly. "I can't help but think Tyler was one of them."

Evan nodded, his expression troubled. "And these posts are a reminder that silence can be deadly. We have to change something before more lives are lost."

Kiera's phone buzzed. It was another message from The Third Rail. This one read:

I am the silence that suffocates. I am the whisper that turns into a roar when you ignore the call for help.

This time, the message was accompanied by an image — a blurred, grayscale photo of a lone figure standing at the edge of a dark hallway. The figure seemed to be reaching out as if pleading for connection. The image struck Kiera deeply; she felt like she was staring into the void where Tyler once stood.

Determined, Kiera suggested, "Let's gather these messages. We need to compile every post and every cryptic word. If we can see the pattern, we can understand what they're trying to tell us."

Evan agreed. Over the next several days, they worked together in the quiet corners of the library. They saved screenshots of every Third Rail post and began to analyze them, searching for common threads or hidden clues. The more they read, the more it became clear that these messages were not random outbursts of anger or grief — they were calculated, desperate expressions of pain silenced by indifference.

During one late-afternoon session, as rain tapped steadily against the library windows, Evan and Kiera poured over the posts. Kiera traced the words with her finger, her eyes soft with tears. "Look at this one," she said, pointing to a post that read, *I wanted to speak, but the world only echoed silence.* "It's like he knew that if we didn't listen, his voice would disappear completely."

Evan leaned back, exhaling slowly. "I keep wondering if, somewhere, Tyler's spirit is still trying to tell us something. If we only paid attention, maybe we could have changed things."

Their shared silence grew heavy with emotion. In that quiet, they realized how much their inaction contributed to the loss. Each post from The Third Rail served as a reminder — a ghostly echo of Tyler's unspoken pain and the price of indifference.

By this time, the posts created a palpable tension within the school. Students began to speak out timidly at first, sharing their experiences of feeling isolated or misunderstood. One afternoon, during a group study session, a freshman timidly admitted, "I always thought my accent and the way I dressed made me weird. I never felt like I belonged, like Tyler did." The confession rippled through the room, and others soon began to share their quiet struggles.

This collective awakening proved both heartening and heartbreaking. It revealed that Tyler's silent suffering was not unique — that the noise of everyday life drowned out countless voices. Some students no longer viewed the posts as a warning but a catalyst for change.

Evan and Kiera realized that the cryptic messages from The Third Rail became a rallying cry. Along with a handful of like-minded students, they resolved to gather more stories, to collect every whispered memory, every hidden regret, and to transform them into a force for change. The school needed to treat every whisper of pain as a call for help and realize only by listening could they create a community where no one would ever feel so alone again.

Chapter 3: The Awakening

The Awakening

The morning light broke softly over River Valley High as if hesitant to reveal the day's secrets. In the stillness of early dawn, the once-muted corridors now promised change. For many students, the past weeks' events carved deep wounds, crying out for healing. But as the day began, a new energy stirred — a subtle yet undeniable sense that something was shifting.

Evan was one of the first to sense it. Sitting by the window in his nearly empty homeroom, he watched as the pale light spilled into the classroom. His notebook lay open before him, filled with scribbled notes and scattered thoughts about Tyler, the lost opportunities, and the new resolve slowly taking shape inside him. He realized the voices of regret and sorrow could no longer be silenced; they cried out to be transformed into something more potent — a call for action.

Earlier that morning, Evan spent long minutes revisiting the archived messages from The Third Rail. In the quiet of his room, he scrolled through each post, each word a raw testament to the anguish allowed to fester. One message, in particular, struck him deeply:

When silence becomes the norm, it's not because we're strong — it's because we've forgotten how to care.

Those words echoed in his mind, as he stared out the window, resolving to no longer let indifference win. He thought of Tyler — a gentle soul whose quiet plea had gone unheard — and vowed to transform his regret ensuring no one else suffered in silence.

In a nearby classroom, Kiera experienced her own awakening. The weight of leadership pressed heavily on her over the past weeks. The constant drive to keep the school together left her emotionally exhausted. Still, the raw memories of Tyler's isolation and the haunting posts from The Third Rail finally forced her to confront a truth she could no longer ignore. Sitting at a desk near an old, sunlit window, Kiera again opened her journal. The pages overflowed with sorrow, determination, and a nascent hope this time.

Every moment we failed him is a call to action, she wrote in a steady hand. *Tyler's silence was not his choice, but our collective failure. Today, I will not let that failure define us. I will fight to create a space where every whisper is heard.*

As the morning advanced, the hallways slowly filled with students whose expressions were etched with a new kind of awareness. Conversations that once centered on mundane topics now veered toward discussions of belonging and identity. A small group of students huddled over a table covered with notebooks and sketches in one corner of the library. They murmured about feeling "invisible," sharing how their differences had often been met with silent judgment. No longer were the walls echoing with judgment and neglect; they now whispered of empathy and change.

At the center of this awakening, Evan and Kiera met again near the lockers. They exchanged a look that was heavy with sorrow and bright with resolve. "We can't keep living in regret," Evan said quietly. "We have to turn our pain into something that saves others."

Kiera nodded, her eyes glistening with determination. "I think we need to reach out — start a conversation with every student who feels unseen. We need to document these stories, not just for ourselves but for the entire community. Let our voices be the antidote to the silence."

Their plan took shape quickly. Kiera and Evan set up a makeshift station in a corner of the library. They placed a large poster with the words "Your Voice Matters" on the wall and provided sticky notes and pens. They encouraged any student passing by to write down a thought, a fear, or a hope — anything that expressed their feelings. The station became a tiny epicenter of raw emotion as the day progressed. Notes ranged from expressions of deep loneliness to quiet affirmations of hope: *I'm tired of being invisible, I'm scared, but I want to be heard,* and *Maybe together, we can be strong.*

Evan collected these notes carefully, aware that each was a story fragment — a piece of a larger mosaic of student life hidden for too long. At that moment, he realized that their initiative was not just about mourning Tyler's death; it was about reclaiming the voices of all those silenced by neglect and bias.

The day's end found the school in a state of hushed transformation. As dusk fell, the corridors were bathed in a gentle, golden light that symbolized a new beginning. The collective actions of the day — the sharing of stories, the handwritten notes, the quiet acts of remembrance — set the stage for something powerful. It was as if the very walls of River Valley High were beginning to whisper back, promising no one would be left to drown in silence ever again.

Evan and Kiera sat together on a set of steps outside the school as the final echoes of the day faded. The notes from the "Your Voice Matters" station had been collected and carefully taped onto a large board. Each message was a testament to a life that struggled and hope not yet extinguished.

"Today felt like the start of something real," Evan said softly, his gaze fixed on the board. "I think we're finally beginning to see what Tyler was trying to tell us — that every silent cry deserves to be heard."

Kiera rested her head against his shoulder. "I know," she murmured. "I feel it in every note, every whispered confession. We can change things — build a community where no one is ever invisible again."

The weight of the day's revelations mingled with the promise of tomorrow. The transformation wasn't complete, and the road ahead was fraught with challenges, but for the first time, there was a sense of unity — a belief that together, they could turn whispers of regret into a resounding chorus of hope.

As the school day ended and the lights dimmed, the echoes of the past mingled with the promise of the future. The long-silenced voices were now beginning to find their strength, and the quiet call for change grew louder. At that moment, Evan and Kiera knew that the journey had just started and that Tyler's memory would forever be the spark igniting a movement for compassion and understanding.

The Deepening of Resolve

In the following days, a transformation began to permeate the halls of River Valley High. It was as if the shared grief of losing Tyler unlocked something within each of them — a desire to reclaim their voices and to stand together against a culture of silence.

Evan returned to the same quiet corner of the library almost every day. He meticulously reviewed every saved post from The Third Rail in that secluded space, away from the bustling crowds and echoing hallways. Each raw, unfiltered message contained a desperate cry cutting straight through his heart. One post, in particular, left an indelible mark on him:

When the world turns its back, your voice becomes a lonely echo. I am that echo, and I beg you — listen.

Evan stared at that post for long minutes, imagining Tyler's frail voice reaching out from the void. The weight of regret pressed down on him like a physical burden. He recalled the quiet afternoons when Tyler would sit by the art room window, lost in thought as if searching for someone who could understand his silent despair. Now, every message from The Third Rail was a reminder of the consequences of inaction.

Across the campus, Kiera was also evolving. The heavy burden of leadership, which had once nearly crushed her, was now transformed into a quiet strength. In a sunlit classroom where the air was filled with the scent of old books and fresh hope, Kiera led a small meeting with a group of students who had begun to gather regularly. They called themselves "The Whisperers," a name encapsulating their shared desire to break the cycle of silence.

During one of these meetings, Kiera stood before the group, her voice steady yet laden with emotion. "I know many of you feel unseen," she began, eyes sweeping over the attentive faces. "For too long, our voices have been drowned out by indifference. But Tyler taught us something precious — that even a whisper can ignite change."

One particularly poignant moment occurred during a small group discussion in a secluded corner of the library, a freshman, who had long hidden behind a wall of timidity, hesitantly confessed, "I come from a small town where everyone always judged you for who you were. I used to feel so ashamed of my accent, my clothes... I felt like I didn't belong anywhere. After everything that's happened, I'm starting to believe maybe I do." His voice was barely audible, but each word carried the weight of years spent in isolation. The group fell silent, each student absorbing the gravity of his admission, his words resonating within each person. In that silence, the room filled with the promise that no one — no matter how different — would ever be overlooked again.

Kiera knelt to meet his gaze, her voice gentle and compassionate. "You belong here exactly as you are," she said firmly. "It's our differences that make us who we are. And I promise you, we're here to listen, to help you find your voice."

The boy's eyes shone with hope, and he nodded slowly. In that moment, the seed of change had taken root — a seed that would grow into a support network, nurtured by every shared story and every act of kindness.

The meeting transformed into a safe space — a refuge where vulnerability was not a weakness but a source of strength. Kiera's heart swelled with hope as she saw the truth of Tyler's legacy reflected in the eyes of her peers. They were no longer willing to remain invisible.

Outside the meeting room, whispers of change began to seep into the broader school culture. Small acts of solidarity emerged: a group of seniors organized an informal "check-in" program, where they would pair up with younger students for lunch, ensuring no one sat alone. Inspired by the shifting tide, a teacher started incorporating discussions of mental health and belonging into her lessons. The once-muted corridors now carried a different cadence — a subtle murmur of collective resolve.

Later that week, during a quiet lunch period under a drizzling sky, Evan and Kiera sat together on the steps outside the school. Evan pulled out the document he'd been compiling, its pages filled with screenshots, handwritten notes, and personal reflections. "Every one of these posts," he said softly, "reminds me that we have a duty — not just to remember Tyler, but to act on the pain his silence represents."

Kiera nodded, her gaze fixed on the document. "We can't let his death be the end of the story," she said. "It's our responsibility to transform that silence into a movement where every whisper is a spark of hope."

At the next "Whisperers" meeting, they discussed practical ways to reach out to the student body. Ideas flowed: a school-wide "Voice Day" where students could share stories openly; a confidential hotline for those in distress; a series of workshops to train peer mentors in active listening and empathy. Every suggestion was a small step toward building a community where no one would ever feel alone again.

As days turned into weeks, the transformation spread like wildfire. The document Evan compiled grew into a digital archive — a collection of anonymous stories, poignant memories, and candid confessions. Students began to volunteer their experiences, each contribution a testament to the collective pain that had once been hidden in silence. The archive became a powerful reminder that their school was not defined by apathy but by the strength of every whisper that dared to be heard.

Late one evening, after a particularly long day of gathering stories and organizing meetings, Kiera and Evan found themselves in the library again. The soft hum of fluorescent lights and the rustle of turning pages provided a quiet backdrop for their reflections. Kiera looked up from her journal, her eyes meeting Evan's, and said, "I keep thinking about that post — the one that said, '*When silence becomes the norm, it's not because we're strong — it's because we've forgotten how to care.*' It's like a mirror, showing us what we've become."

Evan nodded slowly. "I've been wondering if we've been so busy trying to keep everything together that we forgot to listen." He paused, his voice thick with emotion. "Tyler's memory is our wake-up call. We can't let his quiet plea go unheeded any longer."

Together, they vowed to continue their work, not just as a reaction to tragedy but as a commitment to reshaping the culture at River Valley High. Every story they recorded, every note added to the archive, was a promise that the silent voices of the past would become the loud call for change in the future.

As the final bell rang, signaling the end of another school day, the corridors of River Valley High buzzed with a new energy. Initially, the transformation was subtle — small acts of kindness, gentle nods of acknowledgment, and hushed conversations about feeling seen and heard. But beneath it all grew a realization: that change, no matter how quiet, always begins with a single, brave whisper.

Evan and Kiera stepped out into the cool evening air, their hearts lighter and their resolve stronger. They knew the journey ahead was long and fraught with challenges, but they also believed every whispered memory and every shared regret was a steppingstone toward a future where no one would ever have to suffer in silence again.

As darkness fell, the archive of stories glowed softly on Evan's laptop — a beacon of hope, a living testament to the power of vulnerability and connection. And in that glow, he and Kiera found the strength to believe that even in the most profound silence, there is a promise of a new dawn.

The Promise of Change

As dawn settled over River Valley High, a gentle warmth began to seep into the cold corridors that had once echoed with silent despair. The transformations set in motion over the past weeks showed visible signs: lockers adorned with fresh flowers and heartfelt notes, posters bearing messages of hope and solidarity, and clusters of students huddled together in genuine conversation. It was as if the very walls of the school were slowly shedding their old cloak of indifference, revealing instead a tapestry of compassion and unity.

In the early afternoon, the atmosphere outside Tyler's locker had evolved into a quiet celebration of life — a tribute not only to Tyler's lost soul but to the resilience of every student who had ever felt unseen. The once sparsely decorated locker now bore layers of notes in various handwriting styles. Some messages were raw confessions of pain, while others were tender declarations of hope.

One note in bold, looping letters read, *I was seen. I mattered.* Another, written in neat cursive, declared, *Your silence spoke for us. We will never let it be in vain.* The transformation was profound; what had begun as a lonely shrine became a living symbol of change.

In the cafeteria, whispers that had once been full of regret and judgment were now laced with excitement and determination. Groups of students gathered at tables, discussing ideas for a school-wide "Voice Day" — a day when everyone would be invited to share personal stories of struggle and triumph, to celebrate diversity, and the strength found in vulnerability. The energy was palpable, a soft murmur of collective resolve promised to sweep away years of neglect.

In this emerging dialogue, Kiera, Evan and the "Whisperers" continued their quiet work. They spent long hours in the library, gathering stories and whispered memories shared by their peers. Evan recorded each testimony in his laptop as if it were a sacred vow, never to let another silent cry go unheard. Kiera, her eyes often misty with both sorrow and resolve, organized these fragments into a collection that would serve as evidence of the urgent need for change — a living document of the school's collective pain and budding hope.

As the conversation continued, Evan observed how each shared story added to a growing mosaic of resilience. These were not isolated experiences; they were interconnected threads that, when woven together, formed a tapestry of community strength. Kiera looked around and saw that the walls of River Valley High were being transformed — first by the quiet expressions on Tyler's locker and now by the students' voices.

As the session ended, the group made a pact: they would compile these stories and present them to the school board, not as accusations

,but as a call for empathy and change. At that moment, amid the soft glow of library lamps and the rustling of paper, a spark of hope ignited — a hope that silence could be broken, every unanswered question could lead to a future where no one would ever feel so alone.

Kiera and Evan, now recognized as leaders of this emergent movement, greeted the students with a gentle assurance. They encouraged quiet conversations in every corner of the school — from the library's cozy nooks to the outdoor courtyards. With every shared anecdote and every tearful confession, the campus seemed to come alive with a renewed sense of belonging. Even teachers who once regarded mental health with reserved indifference began to engage in more open, heartfelt discussions with their classes. A few even started incorporating brief sessions on empathy and active listening into their lessons, bridging the gap between the administration and the students' lived experiences.

One particular afternoon, as a soft spring rain tapped gently against the windows of the main hall, Kiera organized an impromptu "Voice Circle" right outside the art room. About fifteen students gathered in a rough circle under the shelter of a large oak tree. There was a palpable vulnerability in the air — a mutual understanding every person present had, at some point, felt the sting of isolation.

A timid sophomore, eyes glistening with unshed tears, broke the silence. "I've always felt like I was just background noise," she confessed. "I thought if I stayed quiet, no one would notice my differences. But I'm beginning to see that silence only makes us invisible." Her words, simple and sincere, sent a ripple through the circle. One by one, others shared their own experiences — the sting of a dismissive comment, the pain of being excluded, the moments when they had yearned for someone to notice their quiet struggles.

In that vulnerable space, Kiera listened intently, her heart swelling with sorrow and hope. "Every voice matters," she said softly, addressing the circle. "Tyler's memory isn't just about the loss we feel; it's about the promise that we can make a difference if we dare to speak up. We must honor his legacy by ensuring no one here ever feels alone again."

As the session drew to a close, students left the circle with a newfound sense of unity. Some lingered to share one-on-one, their quiet conversations filled with empathy and understanding. A freshman who had always felt like an outsider because of his modest background expressed how the circle had given him the courage to see that his differences were not something to hide but a source of strength.

In the final moments of the day, as the school's corridors emptied and the last echoes of conversation faded, Kiera stood again by Tyler's locker. Memories of the events washed over her. She recalled the harsh words of bias, the regret of missed opportunities, and now, the gentle voices that dared to rise in defiance of silence. With trembling hands, she retrieved her journal and penned one final line for the day:

Tonight, the whispers have grown into a murmur — a promise that every cry for help will be heard, and no one will ever be forgotten. Once lost in silence, Tyler's voice now echoes in every heart that dares to speak.

As Kiera closed her journal, a soft smile played on her lips. The once dark corridors of River Valley High began to pulse with a new rhythm — a rhythm of hope, connection, and shared courage. The whispers of regret had not disappeared; they had transformed into a collective vow to listen, support, and change. And in that transformation lay the promise of a new dawn where every voice mattered.

Confronting the Past – Revisiting Regret and Responsibility

The hallways of River Valley High had grown accustomed to the soft murmur of change, yet some shadows of the past still lingered like unwelcome ghosts. As the collective momentum swelled, a quieter but more potent current began to rise within the hearts of those who had once felt powerless. For Evan, Kiera, and many of their peers, the time had come to confront the weight of regret and the responsibility that came with the truth of Tyler's silent suffering.

In a secluded corner of the school, a small, neglected conference room that had once been used for meetings, the newly formed group of "Whisperers" gathered. The room, lit by the muted glow of a single overhead light, was transformed into a space where vulnerability was not a weakness but a shared strength. Folding chairs formed a circle, and a whiteboard stood at the front, covered in hastily scribbled notes and questions that none dared to answer.

Evan began the session, his voice low but steady. "We've collected so many stories since Tyler's death," he said, glancing around the circle. "Every one of those stories is a piece of the puzzle. They tell us our silence wasn't just about neglect — it was about fear. Fear of being vulnerable, fear of not fitting in, and fear of confronting our shortcomings."

He paused, allowing his words to sink in. Across the circle, Kiera's eyes glistened with unshed tears as she listened, her mind replaying moments of regret — the times she had been too busy to notice Tyler's quiet pleas and how her ambition blinded her to a friend's pain.

A junior named Marcus, known for his usually quiet demeanor, cleared his throat. "I...I always thought that no one would judge me if I stayed in the background. But looking back, I see how that same silence can hurt. I'm sorry — I'm sorry for all the times I didn't speak up, for all the times I let my fears keep me silent." His voice, though timid, carried a note of sincere contrition.

The admission struck a chord. One by one, other students began to open up, their voices trembling as they recounted memories of being overlooked or failing to act when someone needed them. A sophomore, whose eyes were downcast, confessed, "I used to think that if I didn't make a fuss, I wouldn't be noticed for the wrong reasons. But now I realize that staying silent only deepens the isolation. I wish I'd possessed the courage to help Tyler... or even just to say, 'I'm here for you.'"

At that moment, the room seemed to hold its breath. The atmosphere was thick with the collective recognition that every moment of inaction contributed to a tragedy no one could reverse. Evan's fingers tapped a steady rhythm on the table as he absorbed every word, every confession.

Kiera then took a deep breath and addressed the group, her voice resonating with a blend of sorrow and newfound resolve. "Tyler's life was not defined by his silence but by the unspoken cries we all ignored. Each of us carries a piece of that regret, a fragment of the truth that if we only listened, maybe, just maybe, things would have been different." She paused, letting her words hang in the air. "We owe it to him and ourselves to not let that silence continue. It's time we confront the past, learn from it, and let it guide us toward a future where no one feels invisible."

As the meeting continued, the discussion deepened. They began to reexamine the moments that led to Tyler's isolation. Evan recalled the day after the gym when Tyler had whispered, "I feel like I don't belong here," a confession he had brushed off as fleeting adolescent angst. Now, with painful clarity, he recognized that his dismissal had been a grave mistake — a moment where his inaction had compounded Tyler's loneliness.

One student, who had previously remained silent, raised her hand. "I remember when I noticed Tyler sitting alone after class, sketching. I thought he was just artistic, but now I see he was hiding his pain behind his art." Her honest and unguarded words filled the room with a shared sense of remorse.

The conversation soon turned to the biases that had subtly permeated their environment. Kiera recalled the offhand remarks about Tyler's family — comments that had been dismissed by many as harmless observations but that, in truth, cut deeply into his sense of self-worth. "I overheard a group of students say that Tyler wasn't really 'one of us' because of where he came from," she said softly. "Those words, constantly repeated, create a reality where someone begins to believe they are less than, undeserving of love or belonging."

Ben, who had been notably quiet since his earlier confrontation with Kiera, shifted in his seat. With a hesitance that betrayed his inner conflict, he admitted, "I used to think that kind of comment was just a fact of life. But now...I see that it's not a fact at all. It's a choice — a choice to judge, to isolate, and ultimately, to ignore the humanity in others." His voice was raw with sincerity, and for a moment, the weight of his admission brought tears to his eyes.

The group fell into reflective silence. Each student seemed to be grappling with the shared realization that their inaction — and the biases that allowed them to be indifferent — had real consequences. Evan, feeling the cumulative weight of these revelations, spoke up again. "We've all been part of this silence. But we have the power to break it now. Tyler's memory demands we remember him and learn from our mistakes. We must listen, truly listen, to every cry for help."

The discussion then turned toward concrete actions. Evan opened his laptop and brought up the digital archive they had been compiling — a mosaic of anonymous messages, stories, and reflections documenting River Valley High's shifting culture. Every post and every handwritten note proved a testament to the power of vulnerability and the strength found in a shared community.

"Look at this," Evan said, scrolling through the archive. "Every message is like a tiny spark — tiny sparks that, together, can ignite a blazing fire of change."

Kiera nodded, eyes scanning the pages filled with raw emotion and determination. "It's incredible," she replied. "We started with grief, regret, and fear — and now we're building a future where every voice is valued."

A murmur of agreement ran through the room. Evan's eyes shone with determination as he added, "We should also approach the administration with our findings — not as a weapon, but as a call for change. It's time that everyone understands the cost of silence."

The discussion grew animated as the group fleshed out earlier ideas. They talked about organizing a school-wide event — called "Voice Day" — where every student could share their personal story in an open forum. Some suggested creating safe classroom spaces, while others discussed starting peer support groups that would meet regularly. The energy in the room was electric, and every idea was a tiny spark that contributed to a growing fire.

The atmosphere in the room shifted, growing lighter as the students began to see a way forward. What had started as a collection of regret and pain was now transforming into a shared resolve — a commitment to challenge the status quo and to foster a community where every whisper was valued.

Later that evening, as the group disbanded and the echo of their voices lingered in the empty room, Kiera remained seated at the whiteboard. She stared at the scribbled notes and raw confessions, feeling both sorrow for the past and hope for the future. In the solitude of that moment, she promised herself that she would never let another silent cry go unanswered.

As she stepped into the corridor, Kiera caught sight of a lone student placing a handwritten note on a bulletin board. The note simply read, "I was seen." For a moment, it was as if the entire school breathed a sigh of relief — an acknowledgment that the days of silence were ending.

Outside, the cool night air carried a sense of possibility. Melanie, with a group of students, emboldened by the success of their "Voice Circles", organized an impromptu performance in the courtyard. They recited poetry, sang softly, and even performed a short skit about overcoming isolation. The performance was simple but powerful — a live manifestation of the movement taking root in the heart of their school.

Amid the performance, a banner was unfurled across the front of the stage. In bold letters, it read: *We Are Not Invisible.* The banner, hand-painted by several students as a collaborative effort, was a visual declaration of their collective commitment to change.

In that moment, Kiera felt a surge of emotions — a blend of relief, pride, and a bittersweet recognition of the journey they had all endured. Tyler's memory was no longer a shadow over their lives; it had become the catalyst for a movement transforming their community from within.

After the performance, as students slowly dispersed and the golden light of dusk gave way to a soft, inky night, Kiera walked slowly back toward Tyler's locker. Now a symbol of sorrow and hope, the locker was adorned with fresh flowers and new notes. Scrawled in bold, optimistic letters, one note read, *Your voice saved me*. Another, written in gentle script, said, *Together, we rise*. Each message held a promise — a declaration — that no one would ever face the darkness of isolation again.

Kiera paused, her hand resting lightly on the calm surface of the locker. In that quiet moment, she made a silent vow to herself. "Tyler," she whispered, "your silence has not been in vain. We will carry your light forward until every cry is heard and every whisper becomes a roar."

The new energy was infectious. Over the following days, the transformation at River Valley High grew even more pronounced. Teachers began to host open discussions about mental health and belonging, while the administration cautiously welcomed suggestions from the students. The digital archive of anonymous posts evolved into a living document of change, accessible to anyone who needed a reminder that they were not alone.

By the end of the week, a formal proposal was submitted to the school board — an initiative to incorporate regular "Voice Circles", peer support programs, and a dedicated "Safe Space" corner in the library. This proposal, born from the collective experiences of countless students, was a bold statement that the culture of silence and neglect would no longer be tolerated.

As the final bell of the week rang out, marking the end of another chapter in their shared journey, the corridors of River Valley High pulsed with a renewed sense of purpose. The once-muted voices had found their strength, and the promise of change was no longer a distant dream but a tangible reality built daily.

Chapter 4: The Silent Battle

Seeds of Rebellion

The corridors of River Valley High transformed from cold, indifferent passages into a living, breathing battleground. For weeks, the weight of Tyler's silence, the haunting words of The Third Rail, and the collective grief simmered beneath the surface. Now, as the new semester dawned, that simmering pain prepared to erupt into action.

The school felt different in the early morning light — an undercurrent of tension pulsed through every locker-lined hall. Evan arrived first, his breath visible in the crisp air. He paused at the library's entrance, the familiar building now seeming like a sanctuary for all those who had felt forgotten. Clutching a stack of his notes and the digital archive of anonymous posts, he felt a mix of determination and sorrow. Each message, every desperate cry recorded on his laptop, reminded him of Tyler's quiet anguish and the need for change.

Evan's thoughts wandered to that fateful day when Tyler's voice, barely a whisper, had reached him after the gym. "I feel like I don't belong," Tyler had murmured, and now, Evan's heart broke. Those words were no longer isolated incidents but part of a much larger, aching chorus demanding attention. As a catalyst for change, Evan vowed to transform regret into action and silence into a roar.

Kiera began working in a cramped storage room near the rear of the school. After weeks of relentless meetings, organizing support groups, and enduring the heavy burden of leadership, she learned to channel her grief into a vision for the future. Today, her eyes burned with a fierce resolve as she reviewed the proposals for a new initiative — a school-wide program creating safe spaces for every student, ensuring no one would ever be as unseen as Tyler had been.

Kiera recalled the countless hours spent pouring over journals, the painful introspection as she wrote and rewrote her vows never to let another cry go unanswered. Now, determined to share that commitment with everyone around her, she arranged a small meeting, inviting a group of trusted peers from "The Whisperers" and the Student Support Panel. Their task was straightforward: to lay the groundwork for a movement challenging the entrenched indifference permeating the school.

As the bell rang, signaling the start of the day, students trickled into the room. The atmosphere was thick with anticipation. There was an unspoken understanding among those present: something had to change, and they had the power to make it happen.

Kiera stood before the gathered group, her voice steady despite the turmoil inside her. "We've all felt the loss," she began, her gaze sweeping the room. "Tyler's silence isn't just a memory — it's a call to action. Every whispered note at his locker, every post from The Third Rail, has shown us that our community has failed to see the pain around us."

A murmur of agreement rippled through the group. Evan, sitting near the front, nodded slowly.

"We're here today," Kiera continued, "because we refuse to let that inaction define us. We have a chance — no, a responsibility — to build something new, ensuring every voice is heard, and every cry for help is answered."

The room was silent momentarily, the weight of her words sinking in. Then, a quiet voice from the back spoke up. "But how do we start?" a sophomore asked. "Change seems so big... and we're just a few students."

Kiera smiled, though the strain in her eyes belied the softness of her tone. "Change always starts small," she replied. "It starts with one person deciding that enough is enough. It starts with each of us daring to speak up, to reach out, and to challenge the status quo."

Outside, the school buzzed with energy. In the hallways, students who had once felt isolated now exchanged glances of determination. Groups fragmented by silence were slowly beginning to form bonds over shared experiences. The echoes of regret were transforming into the first notes of a collective rebellion — a movement against a culture that had long ignored the cries of the unseen.

As discussions grew more animated in the meeting room, Evan pulled out his laptop and projected the digital archive onto a blank wall. The screen displayed screenshots of The Third Rail posts — each one a raw, unfiltered account of the pain that had been allowed to fester. A particular post, its words stark and uncompromising, stood out:

When silence becomes the norm, it's not because we are strong — it's because we've forgotten how to care.

The room fell silent as the words hung in the air. For many, that simple statement was a revelation — a mirror reflecting the indifference they had collectively allowed to take root. One by one, students began to share their own stories. A timid freshman spoke of feeling invisible because of his size, while a senior recounted how a teacher's dismissive remark had once made him question his worth.

As each story unfolded, the digital archive became a living testament to the power of vulnerability. The collective confessions, though painful, were also a powerful reminder that they were not alone. Every shared secret, every unspoken regret, added weight to the growing resolve that they would no longer let silence reign.

After the meeting, Kiera and Evan lingered in the room as the group dispersed into the dimming light of late afternoon. The energy was palpable — an undercurrent of hope mixed with a resolve as fierce as it was fragile.

"We have to take this further," Evan said softly, his eyes fixed on the screen. "We can't let these stories stay hidden. They need to be heard by everyone, from the students to the teachers and even the administration."

Kiera nodded. "We'll compile these stories and present them to the school board. It's time that everyone understands the true cost of silence. Tyler's memory should be the spark that lights the way for change."

That evening, as dusk crept over the campus, Evan and Kiera walked side by side along a quiet corridor. Their conversation was low, a mix of hope and sorrow. "I keep thinking," Evan said, "that every moment we ignored him has added to this mountain of regret. But maybe every whispered story can become a steppingstone toward something better now."

Kiera looked ahead, determination etched on her face. "If we keep pushing and fighting for every voice, we can build a community where no one ever feels as alone as Tyler did."

In the soft glow of the hallway lights, they paused at a display near Tyler's locker. Among the fresh flowers and handwritten notes was a new message — a simple, powerful declaration: *I see you. You matter.* The words resonated deeply, a promise that even in the darkest moments, someone would be there to listen.

As they continued their walk, voices swelled around the building. In quiet clusters, students spoke in hushed tones about their dreams, fears, and the small acts of kindness that had already begun to mend the broken silence. It was as if the school was awakening from a long, sorrowful sleep.

Evan and Kiera exchanged a look that said it all — a silent acknowledgment that this was only the beginning of a much larger battle. The road ahead would be long and fraught with challenges, but in that moment, the collective determination of their peers shone through. Every shared story, every confession of pain, was a rallying cry — a call for the transformation of an entire community.

As the night deepened and the corridors finally grew quiet again, Evan returned to the library to continue working on the archive. He spent hours transcribing recordings, organizing messages, and carefully crafting a narrative that would one day be presented to the school board. Each word he typed was a promise — a promise that the voices of the forgotten would not be lost to time.

Kiera, too, found solace in reflection. Sitting by the window in her favorite quiet corner, she reread the journal entries from the day. The raw emotion of every story filled her with both grief and hope. In the gentle light, she realized that the journey toward change was not about erasing the past but honoring it — learning from the pain so that the future could be shaped with compassion and resilience.

By the end of the day, the seed of rebellion had taken firm root in River Valley High. Once a cold arena of whispered indifference, the campus was now alive with murmurs of solidarity. The digital archive glowed softly on Evan's laptop — a mosaic of voices united in the promise of change.

Standing together on the steps outside the school as the final light of day faded, Evan and Kiera felt the weight of their mission. "This is our chance," Evan said quietly. "Every silent cry, every missed opportunity — it's all part of the story we're writing now. And it's a story that demands action."

Kiera squeezed his hand in affirmation. "We're not just reacting to tragedy," she said. "We're building a future where every voice is heard, where every whisper of pain is met with compassion. Tyler's memory is our catalyst, and together, we'll ensure that no one is ever left drowning in silence again."

As the stars emerged overhead, the transformation in the school felt almost tangible — a rising tide of hope that promised to carry them forward into a new dawn.

The Rise of Resistance

As the first light of dawn crept over River Valley High, the quiet rebellion that had begun to stir in the corridors had grown into a palpable current. The seeds of change planted in the wake of Tyler's death were now sprouting in unexpected places — within whispered conversations in the library, in the determined glances exchanged between students, and even in the tentative support emerging from previously indifferent teachers.

In the early hours of that fateful morning, Evan arrived at school with an intensity that had become his burden and fuel. The digital archive of anonymous posts, which he had meticulously compiled since the days following Tyler's passing, glowed softly on his laptop as he stepped into the nearly empty hallway. Every message from The Third Rail, served as a stark reminder of the consequences of indifference. Today, however, those messages evolved into a clarion call for resistance.

Evan's thoughts drifted back to the haunting words of one post:

When silence becomes the norm, it's not because we are strong — it's because we've forgotten how to care.

As he walked through the corridors that morning, he saw something that sparked his resolve even further. A hand-painted and vibrant banner had been unfurled on the notice board near the main entrance. In bold letters, it read:

Break the Silence. Let Every Voice Be Heard.

The banner was simple yet powerful, and it had been crafted by a group of seniors who had grown tired of the same old excuses and neglect. Evan paused to absorb the message, feeling his heart race with hope and urgency. This was more than just a piece of art — it was a manifesto, a declaration that the time for passive acccptance was over.

In a classroom near the main hall, Kiera led a secret meeting with the "Whisperers", a diverse group of students hailing from all walks within the school: jocks, tech geeks, nerds, fashionistas, band members, glee club, and more. To Kiera's surprise, Ben took a chair at the table, nodding to her as the rest gathered around a makeshift table, expressions serious as they began discussing their next steps. Kiera's voice, though steady, carried the weight of her internal struggles.

"We've seen what happens when no one listens," she said firmly, "and we cannot allow it to continue. Tyler's memory is not just a reminder of our failure — it is a challenge to all of us. We must transform our collective pain into action."

A sophomore, eyes downcast but determined, added, "I've been feeling invisible for so long, but now is the time to step up and be seen. It's not just about me — all of us who have been pushed aside."

Meanwhile, beyond the secret meetings and hushed gatherings, the ripple effects of resistance began to surface in unexpected ways. A history teacher, Mr. Hernandez, who had long maintained a stoic silence regarding student struggles, began incorporating discussions on empathy and social justice into his lectures. His classroom, once strictly focused on dates and events, now buzzed with conversations about how history was shaped not just by the powerful but by every individual who dared to challenge injustice.

In the cafeteria, the atmosphere had noticeably shifted. Once dominated by gossip and apathy, small groups huddled together, discussing their plans for change. At one table, Melanie explained how she had used her art class to create a series of posters that celebrated diversity and highlighted the importance of listening. "I realized that if we can see beauty in our differences, we can learn to value every voice," she said passionately, her eyes alight with determination.

Even the school's administration began to take note. Rumors of student-led initiatives and growing unrest reached the ears of Principal Chapman. In a rare move, he called for a meeting with several teachers and a few student representatives. In the cramped conference room, the air was thick with tension. Principal Chapman, who had previously dismissed many students' concerns, now faced a united front.

"We are not ignoring the issues any longer," one of the teachers said, her voice firm. "There's a growing movement among the students — a demand for change that we can't afford to overlook."

One student representative, a resolute junior, spoke up, "We're tired of being told that our pain doesn't matter. Tyler's memory reminds me that every whisper of hurt should be cared for. We need real change, not just empty promises."

The meeting ended with a sense of reluctant acknowledgment from the administration. Principal Chapman's stern expression softened as he promised to "look into" the matter. But for the students, this was just the beginning; they knew that meaningful change would require persistence and courage far beyond polite assurances.

Outside, the rain had finally ceased, leaving a cool, clean night air that seemed to signal a fresh start. The once-somber corridors of River Valley High now pulsed with the promise of a new dawn. Groups of students emerged from the library and classrooms, whispering excitedly about "Voice Day" and other initiatives. Once a silent repository of pain, the digital archive had transformed into a living testament to the power of collective action.

At that moment, as the campus buzzed with the promise of change and the silent revolution gathered strength, the bonds between the students solidified. They were no longer just individuals bearing their burdens — they had become a united force, ready to stand up against the systemic indifference that had long allowed suffering to go unnoticed.

Every whispered story, every note added to the archive, and every heartfelt conversation was a testament to their growing resilience. The rise of this collective voice was not just a reaction to tragedy — it was a bold declaration that every student at River Valley High mattered. And as the final echoes of the day's discussions faded into the night, the promise of change burned brightly in every heart present.

Confronting the System

The transformation at River Valley High was no longer confined to whispered conversations or secret meetings — it had reached a boiling point. The persistent calls for change, fueled by the collective grief and determination of the students, evolved into a direct challenge to the very system that allowed Tyler's suffering to go unnoticed. This was when anger, regret, and hope converged into action, demanding the administration face its shortcomings head-on.

Evan arrived at school with a renewed determination, his laptop cradled under his arm, its screen filled with the digital archive of every Third Rail post and every whispered confession collected over the past weeks. The archive was no longer just a repository of sorrow

— it had become evidence, a manifesto of the students' collective experience.

Evan's heart pounded as he approached the administration wing. The air was thick with tension. Posters bearing slogans such as *No More Silence!* and *Our Voices Matter* were prominently displayed, directly challenging the institution's previous indifference. It was clear to everyone that the students were not content with half-hearted promises and empty platitudes.

Inside a sterile conference room with a long-polished table and an atmosphere heavy with expectation, Principal Chapman, along with several department heads and counselors, gathered for an emergency meeting. Rumors circulated about the growing unrest, and today, they would finally face the students' demands.

Kiera entered the room with a calm yet determined stride. She took a deep breath before addressing the assembled administrators. "Thank you for meeting with us," she began, her voice clear and unwavering despite the emotion behind her words. "We are not here to cast blame indiscriminately; we are here to share the truth of what has been happening in our school. These are not isolated incidents but symptoms of a deeper, systemic failure that we can no longer ignore."

She motioned toward the projector screen behind her. On it, the digital archive played in a continuous loop: screenshots of The Third Rail posts, images of Tyler's locker adorned with flowers and handwritten notes, and short video clips of students sharing their confessions in hushed, tearful tones. One clip, in particular, featured a freshman whose soft voice trembled as he said, "I always felt invisible. I'm tired of being ignored."

A heavy silence descended upon the room as the administrators absorbed the raw evidence. Principal Chapman cleared his throat and spoke in a measured tone. "We understand that there are concerns," he said cautiously, "but you must also understand that our protocols are in place to ensure the safety and well-being of all students."

Kiera's eyes flashed with determination. "Protocols?" she countered. "How many cries for help have been met with empty assurances? Tyler's memory isn't just a statistic; it's a testament to how our current system has allowed neglect and indifference to flourish. We have documented students who felt isolated, ignored, and pressured to conform. These are not mistakes — they are systemic failures."

As murmurs arose from some department heads, Evan took a deep breath and added, "Every message we've collected tells a story — a story of a community that has forgotten how to care. We believe change is not only possible but necessary. It starts with acknowledging that our silence has cost us dearly."

For several moments, the room was engulfed in silence. The tension was almost tangible; every administrator seemed to wrestle with the undeniable truths before them. Finally, one of the department heads, a seasoned counselor with years of experience, spoke. "I admit," she said slowly, "that we have overlooked many of these issues. But our budget, our policies... they constrain us. Change doesn't happen overnight."

Kiera's gaze hardened. "Constraints are no excuse for inaction," she replied. "Tyler's death is a direct result of our failure to adapt. We need reform — not just superficial changes, but a fundamental shift in how this school responds to the cries for help that echo through its halls."

At that moment, the atmosphere in the room shifted. Some administrators exchanged uneasy glances, while others remained stoically silent. Principal Chapman's face tightened as he tried to regain control. "We will review this evidence and consider appropriate measures," he said, but the words sounded hollow to the determined faces in the room.

Outside, the students waiting in the corridor could sense the gravity of the confrontation. The meeting, though unresolved, was a pivotal moment — a first step toward holding the system accountable. In the following days, the students intensified their efforts. A group of peers began drafting an official petition demanding that the administration implement a comprehensive review of mental health policies and invest in resources that genuinely support the vulnerable.

Evan and Kiera worked tirelessly, gathering additional testimonies and refining their presentation. They organized small workshops and "Voice Circles" to empower more students to share their stories.

Each session added to their growing archive — a digital tapestry of pain and resilience that could no longer be ignored.

One afternoon, as Kiera and Evan met with several student representatives in the now-transformed library, a quiet junior spoke up, his voice steady despite the lingering fear. "I've felt ignored for so long because I come from a modest background. I've always been told to keep my head down and not cause trouble. But now, listening to all these stories, I realize that silence only hurts us more." His words were simple yet carried a powerful message, resonating deeply with everyone present.

Kiera looked around the room, seeing determination and vulnerability on every face. "We are here to ensure that no one's story is left untold," she said. "We want to build a future where every cry for help is answered, where every whisper is transformed into a voice that can't be silenced."

The discussion soon evolved into concrete plans. They debated organizing a public forum — an event they tentatively called "The Voice Unbound" — where students, teachers, and parents could discuss these issues openly. They discussed the need for peer support groups, creating a dedicated digital platform for anonymous confessions, and even forming a committee to monitor and report on the school's mental health policies. Though tentative, each idea added another layer to their resolve.

During this planning, the digital archive continued to grow. Every new post from The Third Rail — each one a raw expression of pain and defiance — served as a constant reminder of why they were fighting. One post in particular resonated with many:

When silence is all you know, every unanswered cry becomes a wound that never heals. We demand that you listen.

This was not just a plea but a battle cry — a declaration that the status quo could no longer be maintained.

Kiera and Evan entered the cool evening air once the meeting wound down. The corridors, now illuminated by the soft glow of streetlights, felt like a different world — a world on the brink of change. The collective determination of the students had sparked a fire that was beginning to light the darkness.

Evan looked over at Kiera, his eyes reflecting both the weight of their mission and the faint glimmer of hope. "We have a lot of work ahead of us," he said quietly, "but tonight, I feel like every silent voice is finally starting to find its strength."

Kiera nodded. "Tyler's memory will never be erased by silence. We owe it to him — and to everyone else who's felt unseen — to keep pushing for a future where every cry for help is answered."

At that moment, as the night deepened and the school's corridors grew quiet again, the movement to confront the system had taken on a life of its own. Every collected story, every whispered confession, was a testament to a community rising against years of indifference. The challenge before them was immense, but so was their resolve.

The confrontation with the system was not a single moment but a process — a gradual, relentless push toward accountability and change. With every meeting, every public forum, and every new story added to their archive, the students of River Valley High were carving out a new reality. One in which silence would no longer be a haven for indifference but a battleground where every voice, no matter how soft, was celebrated as a call for change.

The Final Stand – Voices in Unity

The pressure had been building for weeks. Every whispered secret, every note left at Tyler's locker, and anonymous post from The Third Rail converged into a singular, relentless call for change. Now, standing on the precipice of transformation, the River Valley High students prepared for their final stand. At this moment, unity would become their most potent weapon against systemic neglect.

It began on a cool, crisp morning. The campus, which had long been a stage for quiet suffering and hidden pain, was abuzz with tangible energy — a simmering anticipation that something monumental was about to unfold. In the days leading up to this moment, the efforts of The Whisperers and the countless voices they gathered coalesced into a plan: a public demonstration that would force the school's administration and community to confront the long-ignored issues of mental health, bias, and indifference.

Evan arrived early at the main entrance, his laptop again his constant companion. The digital archive of collected stories and posts was now evidence of a failing system and a manifesto of their shared hope.

As he walked through the corridors, his eyes caught sight of a large banner draped across the auditorium entrance. Bold, resolute letters declared: "Our Voices Will Not Be Silenced." The message pulsed with defiant energy, a promise that the movement was unstoppable.

In the gathering storm, Kiera made her way to the auditorium, where a sea of students had assembled. The air was heavy with determination, and every face reflected a mixture of sorrow and unwavering resolve. The auditorium, usually a place for routine assemblies and rehearsals, had been transformed into a form of raw, collective power. Chairs were arranged in concentric circles, and a small stage had been set up — its simplicity a testament to the grassroots nature of the movement.

Kiera took a moment at the back of the room, gathering her thoughts. She recalled every regret that had haunted her since Tyler's death — the times when she had been too busy, too blinded by her responsibilities to see the quiet anguish of a friend. Now, those moments fueled her determination. She thought of Tyler's gentle smile, his silent pleas, and the profound loneliness that had driven him to vanish without a proper goodbye.

Taking a deep breath, she stepped onto the stage. The murmur of the crowd softened as all eyes turned to her. "Today," she began, her voice resonating clearly through the microphone, "we stand here not just in memory of Tyler but as a declaration that we will no longer allow silence to be our default. We are the voices that will shatter the indifference that has hidden so many of us. Each one of you, every single cry for help that has been ignored, is a spark — and together, we will ignite a flame of change that cannot be extinguished."

A hushed murmur of agreement ran through the audience. Standing near the front, Evan felt tears welling up as he recalled Tyler's words that he had once so carelessly dismissed. Those words echoed back with a piercing clarity: "I feel like I don't belong..." They were no longer just his lament; they were a rallying cry for every student who had ever felt invisible.

As Kiera continued, the students began to share their own stories. One by one, brave voices rose in the auditorium — a freshman tearfully recounted the isolation she felt due to her religion; a senior described feeling ostracized for his family's political beliefs; and even a usually quiet junior spoke of the pain he suffered being a migrant – far from his home country. Each testimony was interwoven with the shared memory of Tyler — a reminder that his silent struggle was not an isolated tragedy but part of a much larger narrative.

The air grew electric with the power of vulnerability. The auditorium was filled with tears, nods, and murmurs of support. For the first time in a long while, the collective determination to be seen and heard lifted the oppressive weight of indifference. The stage became a platform where personal pain transformed into collective strength — where every whispered memory contributed to a louder, unified voice.

After the testimonies, Kiera invited the audience to participate in a moment of silence — a tribute not only to Tyler but to every soul that had ever suffered in silence. The room fell into a profound hush, the only sound the quiet, synchronized breathing of hundreds of hearts united in grief and hope. There was a promise in that silence: that no one would ever be forgotten, every cry would be met with compassion, and that the era of indifference was ending.

Following the moment of silence, Evan took the stage. "We have documented every story," he said, gesturing to the digital archive now projected onto a large screen behind him. "Every post, every note, is a reminder that our community has been crying out for help for far too long. It's time we turned those cries into a call for action. We are here to demand accountability from our school administration and to ensure that the system that failed Tyler — and so many others — undergoes real, lasting change."

The administration, which had been quietly monitoring the event, could no longer ignore the tide of emotion and the power of the collective voice. Principal Chapman, his face a mask of apprehension and regret, stood up as the murmurs in the room swelled into determined shouts. "I hear you," he said, his voice barely rising above the din. "We will review the evidence and work with you to create a system that truly cares." Though his words did little to quiet the storm of demands, they marked the beginning of an acknowledgment — another step toward dismantling the barriers that had silenced too many voices.

As the event concluded and the auditorium slowly emptied, Kiera and Evan stood together on the stage. The lights dimmed, and only the soft glow of the projector remained, illuminating the faces of those who had come together to break the silence. Evan's eyes met Kiera's, and in that shared glance, there was an unspoken promise — a commitment to carry forward the legacy of every unheard cry and every silent plea.

"This is just the beginning," Kiera whispered, her voice trembling with emotion. "We have turned our grief into action, but there is still much more to do. Tyler's memory must be the spark that lights our way forward."

Evan nodded, his voice resolute despite the lingering sorrow. "Every story we share, every whisper that becomes a shout, brings us one step closer to a future where no one is left unseen."

The auditorium, now empty but echoing with the residual energy of the event, stood as a testament to the power of unity. In that final, transformative moment, the students of River Valley High had not only confronted the system that had failed them — they had also forged a community where every voice mattered, where every cry for help was a catalyst for change.

As the forum drew to a close, the impact of the day's events was evident in every face in the auditorium. The collective act of speaking out had shattered the long-held culture of silence. In the days that followed, the movement grew rapidly. The digital stories archive became a permanent fixture on the school's website. The new initiatives envisioned by the "Whisperers" were launched — peer support groups, regular "Voice Circles," and a dedicated online platform where students could share their thoughts anonymously yet safely.

In the corridors outside, the transformation was unmistakable. Groups of students, once huddled in isolation, now gathered in clusters, their conversations animated and supportive. Teachers who had once dismissed the topic of mental health now engaged in open discussions with their classes. The very atmosphere of River Valley High had shifted from one of quiet despair to one of burgeoning hope and collective responsibility.

As the night deepened, the campus settled into a quiet calm. Yet the promise of a new dawn lingered in the air — a promise born from the strength of a collective voice determined to shatter the silence forever.

The Turning Point

As the final days of the confrontation with the system passed, a palpable shift began to ripple through the halls of River Valley High. The campus, once burdened by silent despair and entrenched indifference, now hummed with newfound energy — a mixture of cautious optimism and defiant resolve. Every whispered conversation, every small act of rebellion, and every shared story had coalesced into a force that could no longer be ignored.

Students gathered near the main entrance on a brisk morning, with the sky a clear expanse of hopeful blue. The banners from previous weeks had been replaced with newer ones, bold and unyielding. One banner stretched across the wall, proclaiming in large, vibrant letters: *Rise, Speak Out, Stand Together*. This slogan had quickly become the rallying cry of the movement, a reminder that every voice mattered and that collective action was the key to breaking the silence.

During this transforming environment, Kiera and Evan stood together on the steps outside the administration building. Their faces, marked by both sorrow and determination, told the story of a journey that had been long and arduous — but one that was now bearing fruit. Around them, students moved with purpose. Some discussed plans for upcoming initiatives, while others shared quiet words of encouragement. The atmosphere was one of renewal, as if the very spirit of the school was being reborn through their united efforts.

Kiera recalled the early days when her heart ached at every neglected cry and every unheeded plea. Now, that same heartbeat with a steady rhythm of resolve. "We've done more than we ever imagined," she said softly to Evan as they watched a group of juniors pass by, laughing and talking animatedly. "Tyler's memory... it's not just a wound anymore. It's become our compass — a reminder of what we must build together."

Evan nodded, his gaze drifting to the digital archive displayed on his tablet. "Every story, every note on Tyler's locker, and post from The Third Rail are not just memories of pain. They're the blueprint for change." His voice was low but firm, carrying the weight of his transformation and the collective hope that had emerged from the tragedy.

Across the campus, efforts to institutionalize this change were beginning to show results. In classrooms where teachers had once dismissed discussions of mental health, new programs were being introduced. A counselor, once hesitant to speak openly about the issues, now led weekly sessions on emotional well-being. Peer-led support groups met regularly in the library, and the "Voice Day" initiative sparked a school-wide conversation about belonging and empathy.

The change was visible in the small interactions that had become the norm in the cafeteria. A group of students who had once sat in isolated corners now shared tables without hesitation. A teacher walked by and paused to ask a student if they were okay — something that would have been unthinkable before. The corridors, once echoing with quiet judgment, now resonated with gentle greetings and affirmations of support.

One afternoon, during a particularly lively "Voice Circle" held under a sprawling oak tree in the courtyard, a student named Aaron stood up and addressed the group. "I used to feel like I didn't matter," he began, his voice wavering with emotion. "Every day, I thought I was invisible because I was different, I go to special classes. But today, I stand here and know that my voice is a part of something bigger — a community that refuses to let anyone be left behind." His words, filled with raw honesty, were met with a round of quiet applause and nods of understanding. It was a moment that encapsulated the transformation that had taken root — a shift from isolation to inclusion, from silence to sound.

Meanwhile, Kiera worked tirelessly to ensure the movement's momentum did not wane. She spent hours coordinating with teachers, student leaders, and even sympathetic administrators to draft a proposal for comprehensive reforms. This proposal, which detailed actionable steps to address mental health, reduce bias, and foster a culture of open dialogue, was to be presented to the school board within the next few weeks. Kiera knew that while the initial uprising had been spontaneous, lasting change required structure and commitment.

In a quiet meeting later that week, she and Evan reviewed the proposal together in the hushed ambiance of the library. Evan scrolled through pages of collected testimonies and carefully collated data while Kiera annotated each point with determination and hope. "This isn't just about Tyler," she said, her voice steady. "It's about every student who has ever felt unheard or unseen. We're not just demanding change — we're building it."

Evan's eyes shone as he replied, "And this is only the beginning."

Outside, as the final school day of the term drew near, the campus seemed to pulse with an energy that was both invigorating and bittersweet. The legacy of Tyler, once a symbol of silent suffering, had become the catalyst for a sweeping change. Every corner of the school bore witness to the transformation: the renovated common areas were filled with art created by students, the library now featured a dedicated section for personal stories and reflections, and the digital archive had become a living repository of hope, accessible to all who needed a reminder that they mattered.

On the eve of graduation, a final, celebratory event was organized —

a culmination of all their efforts, aptly named "The Night of Echoes." Held in the school auditorium, the event was a vibrant showcase of art, poetry, and music. Students took the stage to share their stories, recite poems, and perform songs celebrating the journey from silence to sound. Amid the laughter, tears, and heartfelt applause, the movement was immortalized as a force for good — a living tribute to Tyler's memory and a promise never to let anyone fade into the background again.

At the climax of the evening, as the last notes of a soulful melody faded into the night, Kiera took the stage one final time. "Tonight," she said, her voice resonating with quiet authority, "we celebrate not just the end of our time at River Valley but the beginning of a future defined by empathy, resilience, and the unyielding belief that every voice matters. Tyler's silence gave birth to our movement, and today, we honor that legacy by continuing to speak out, to reach out, and to stand together — no matter where life takes us."

The crowd erupted into applause, their cheers echoing as a promise of continuity. At that moment, under a sky filled with stars, every individual present understood that they were part of something greater than themselves — a collective legacy of hope, resilience, and transformation.

As the final light of day faded into the gentle embrace of night, Evan and Kiera knew that their journey was far from over. But in the transformation around them — the vivid murals, the heartfelt testimonies, and the united voices echoing in every corridor — they saw a future where every cry would be met with compassion, the sound of solidarity would break every silence, and no one would ever again be left drowning in the dark.

Chapter 5: The New Horizon

Rebirth of Hope

As the final days of high school slipped away, the campus of River Valley High was a study in contrasts. The once-cold corridors now buzzed with the promise of new beginnings. The digital archive that Evan had built, once a somber collection of grief, was transforming into a beacon of possibility. The posters, the "Voice Circles," and even the simple, heartfelt notes left at Tyler's locker all contributed to a shift in culture — from isolation to connection, from silence to sound.

Evan, Kiera, Ben, and Melanie — each carrying the weight of Tyler's memory in their own way — found themselves at a crossroads. They had ignited a movement within the school that transformed silent whispers into a chorus of voices demanding that every cry for help be answered. But as summer loomed, a question emerged: What comes next?

The student leaders gathered in a late-night meeting in the school's auditorium to plan their next steps. The room was filled with an electric energy of nervous anticipation and unwavering resolve. Evan projected the digital archive onto a large screen, and as the soft light illuminated the faces of his peers, he spoke with quiet authority.

"Tyler's legacy is not one of silence — it's a call to action. Every story we've collected is a testament to the pain of being unseen, but it's also a reminder that change is possible. We can share these voices and build a community where no one is forgotten."

Her voice steady and resolute, Kiera added, "Our journey doesn't end here at River Valley High. We're on the brink of something much larger — a movement that will carry our stories, hope, and promise into the world beyond these walls. We must use the lessons we've learned here to create spaces where every whisper is a steppingstone to a better future."

The meeting continued for hours, with each student contributing ideas, plans, and personal commitments. They discussed launching a digital campaign, hosting community forums, and partnering with local organizations to spread their message. Every suggestion was met with enthusiastic nods and the realization that they were no longer powerless — they had become a united front determined to reshape the world around them.

As the meeting drew to a close, the participants left the auditorium with renewed purpose. Once a mere backdrop for their daily struggles, the campus became the starting point of a much larger journey. The rising momentum among the students was palpable; it was as if every conversation, shared story, and act of defiance had coalesced into a powerful force.

That night, under a sky filled with countless stars, Evan sat on the roof of an abandoned building near campus, his laptop open as he worked on the next phase of the digital archive. He reflected on the transformation that had taken root in the past few weeks. "This is just the beginning," he whispered to himself, "a new horizon where every voice matters, and every whisper becomes a part of our collective song."

For Evan, the answer lay in his burgeoning passion for storytelling. Every night in his small room, lit by the glow of his laptop, he compiled the digital archive of anonymous posts, testimonies, and personal reflections into what he called "The Echoes Project." It was more than a mere record of loss; it was a living document of every hidden pain and every quiet act of rebellion. Evan believed these stories held the power to reach beyond the confines of River Valley High to inspire change in communities far more prominent than their own.

One sweltering morning, as he sat on the steps outside the library, Evan scrolled through his archive. The posts from The Third Rail had once filled him with regret; now, they ignited within him a fierce resolve. "We have to share this with the world," he muttered. "Tyler's silence is not the end — it's the beginning." With that, he began drafting ideas for a podcast series that would give voice to the forgotten and challenge indifference wherever it reigned.

Melanie, too, felt the pull of the future. In the final weeks before graduation, she wrestled with a profound, transformative question: How could she, a once-overwhelmed student, harness her pain and channel it into genuine change? During one late evening, Melanie sat in her favorite corner of the art room. Surrounded by canvases and sketches, she began to paint. Her brush moved slowly, almost meditatively, across the canvas as she poured her emotions into every stroke. With each layer of paint, she felt the heavy burden of responsibility lighten just a little. She knew that her role wasn't just to aid the movement but to pave the way for a future where every student would feel seen and valued, no matter where they came from.

Melanie, whose quiet strength had blossomed in the safe space of the "Voice Circles", was ready to take her message beyond the confines of her familiar circles. "Voice Circles" grew into a vibrant forum where students discussed literature, shared personal experiences, and found the courage to speak about their deepest fears. Inspired by the success of those sessions, Melanie envisioned a community-wide initiative — a festival of voices where art, poetry, and music would celebrate the diversity of experiences and affirm the belief that every individual mattered. She spent long hours drafting plans for what she tentatively called "The Festival of Echoes," a day-long event that would bring together students, teachers, and even local community members. In her mind, the festival would be a memorial to Tyler, a tribute to every whispered cry that had once gone unnoticed, and a declaration that from silence could rise a powerful, collective song of hope.

In one of her quieter moments, Kiera recalled a conversation with her late mentor. This teacher had taught her that authentic leadership was about empowering others rather than bearing the weight of every problem. "You must learn to let go," her mentor had said, "not to abandon your responsibilities, but to trust that your community will rise to the occasion if you give them space." Kiera had struggled with that advice for so long. But now, with graduation on the horizon and the movement growing ever stronger, she began to see that letting go didn't mean losing control — it meant opening the door for a new kind of leadership, one where every voice had a chance to be heard.

Walking home slowly under the glow of streetlights, Kiera's mind raced with plans and possibilities. She thought of the student who had bravely confessed his loneliness because of his gender identity, the junior who had shared how she felt ignored due to her appearance, and the quiet determination in the eyes of every member of The Whisperers. She saw the future in those faces — where their community would rise from the ashes of silence and build something unbreakable together.

Ben, whose guilt once seemed insurmountable, found solace in unexpected places. While the others worked within the school, Ben volunteered in the middle school as a teacher's aide. In the summer, he volunteered at a local community center. He began to see that his journey toward forgiveness was part of a larger tapestry of healing. Working with younger kids gave him the opportunity to help them build their self-worth and provide them with an older kid to look up to and lean on. Ben discovered that every act of kindness — no matter how small — was a step toward redemption. In the community center's sunlit room, surrounded by laughter and shared stories, he felt that the ghosts of his past were slowly giving way to a future defined by hope rather than regret. "Maybe I can help others," he thought, "and in doing so, finally forgive myself for the times I fell short." As he helped a young boy with a puzzle and listened to the child's small voice recount a difficult day at school, he felt the heavy chains of his past begin to loosen. At that moment, he understood that every act of kindness was a step toward healing and forgiving himself and the system that had failed them all.

Turning Passion into Action

The transformation that began within the walls of River Valley High was not meant to be contained within its corridors. After graduation, Evan, Kiera, Ben, and Melanie realized their shared journey was just the beginning — a spark that could ignite a broader movement. The ideas and emotions nurtured during those intense, formative months were ready to burst into tangible action, setting the stage for change far beyond the campus.

On a warm summer afternoon, the group gathered in the old community center — a space that had long served as a haven for quiet meetings and whispered dreams. The worn-out seats, once a reminder of forgotten classes, now bore witness to the birth of a new chapter in their lives. The atmosphere was charged with an electric anticipation, as if every corner of the room pulsed with the promise of transformation.

Evan opened his laptop and projected the digital archive onto the large screen at the front of the meeting room. The images were a mosaic of every Third Rail post, every note left at Tyler's locker, and every personal story they had collected. It was a visual testimony to the power of voices once lost in silence. As the images scrolled slowly, Evan's voice resonated through the room.

"We've gathered these stories as a reminder of what happened here," he said, his tone steady yet imbued with deep emotion. "But they're also a call to action. We cannot let our grief remain confined to these walls. Tyler's memory and every silent cry must fuel our efforts to make a difference in the wider community."

Kiera stepped forward, her gaze sweeping the room. "Over the past months, we've witnessed the power of vulnerability and collective strength," she continued. "Our journey started with painful regret and a promise to honor Tyler's legacy. Today, we stand ready to transform those lessons into real change. We are prepared to reach out to our community, to work with local organizations, and to create programs that ensure every voice, no matter how quiet, is given the space to be heard."

Her words were met with a mixture of nods and determined stares. The discussion that followed was intense and fervent. Ideas flew around the room like sparks — concepts for community workshops, support groups for at-risk youth, and collaborations with local artists to create public memorials that celebrated resilience and hope.

Evan, Ben, Kiera and Melanie laid out their individual plans for the group.

Ben, who had once struggled under guilt, now spoke confidently. "Working at the community center taught me that change starts with small acts," he explained. "I've seen how a simple conversation or a small gesture of kindness can heal deep wounds. I believe we can replicate that on a larger scale here. We can create a network — a chain of support that connects our school to the community, ensuring that no one is left to suffer in silence."

Evan discussed his vision of a future where the digital archive, which had once been a personal repository of sorrow, would become a resource for other schools grappling with similar issues. He dreamed of partnerships with local non-profits, mental health centers, and community organizations that could help amplify their message.

Melanie, whose journey in the "Voice Circles" blossomed into a passion for creative expression, shared her vision next. "Imagine a festival of voices," she said, her eyes excitedly shining. "A day when the whole community comes together to share art, poetry, music — every expression of the human experience. It would celebrate diversity, a tribute to every whisper overlooked. We can call it 'The Festival of Echoes' — a memorial to Tyler and a symbol of our collective strength."

The room erupted into thoughtful chatter as the group sketched concrete plans. They discussed partnerships with local nonprofits, the possibility of securing a grant to support mental health programs, and ways to involve parents and teachers in this growing movement. Every suggestion was carefully considered and refined, each building block for what would soon become a community-wide initiative.

Outside the auditorium, the buzz of the movement spread like wildfire. Posters promoting "The Festival of Echoes" began appearing on community bulletin boards, and social media pages lit up with messages of support. The digital archive, once a private repository of sorrow and regret, was gradually opened up to the public — transforming into an online platform where people from across the city could read the stories and share their own experiences of isolation, resilience, and hope.

In one particularly memorable meeting at the local community center, Evan and Kiera joined forces with a small group of local youth leaders. The room was modest — a converted classroom in a community building with peeling paint and worn-out chairs — but the energy within was undeniable. The discussion that unfolded was raw and unfiltered. Young people from various neighborhoods spoke of their struggles with feeling marginalized, encountering biases in everyday life, and the transformative power of simply being heard.

A girl from a nearby neighborhood, trembling with fear and determination, said, "I've always felt that my background made me an outsider. I was constantly reminded that I didn't fit in. But here, listening to your stories, I feel like maybe I belong somewhere." Her words, echoing the experiences of so many, were met with supportive nods and gentle smiles.

Kiera, taking in the collective stories, felt a surge of resolve. "This is why we're doing this," she said passionately. "It's not just about our school. It's about every person who's ever felt invisible. We have the power to change that — to create a community where every cry for help is met with a compassionate hand, where every whispered fear is answered with understanding."

As the meeting drew to a close, plans were set in motion. A team was formed to launch the online platform, and commitments were made to host community forums in the coming months. The digital archive, now rebranded as "The Echoes Project," would serve as the backbone of this movement — a living testament to the power of collective memory and action.

Evan found a quiet moment as the group disbanded and the community center's lights dimmed late that evening. Sitting at a corner table with his laptop open, he reflected on the journey thus far. Every story he had collected, every post he had saved, was a reminder of the fragility and the strength of the human spirit. "This is our turning point," he whispered to himself. "We are no longer just a school reacting to tragedy — we are a community taking control of our future."

The movement was gathering momentum, not only in River Valley High but in the broader community. Every conversation, every shared memory, was a step toward a future where the echoes of the past would serve as a guide — not a chain to hold them back. With every piece of evidence from The Third Rail, every heartfelt note from a student, the resistance solidified into a collective force determined to transform not only their school but also the culture of the community at large.

In that pivotal moment, as the town continued to hum with the energy of united voices and shared determination, Evan, Kiera, and their peers knew their work was just beginning. The transformation that had taken root in the corridors of River Valley High was destined to spread far beyond its walls. With every whispered confession and every act of defiance, they were writing a new narrative where every voice was valued, every cry was heard, and the power of connection finally replaced silence.

And so, as the night deepened and the last remnants of the day's energy faded into a serene calm, the promise of change shone brightly. The Echoes Project was more than an archive — it was a declaration that every story mattered and that they could reshape the future together. In the quiet determination of a community reborn, the movement was ready to carry the legacy of Tyler into a new dawn — a dawn defined by hope, unity, and the unwavering belief that no one would ever be left unheard again.

Consolidating the Future – Embracing Leadership

Kiera took on a more strategic role within the movement. The intense period of grassroots organizing taught her that passion was essential but needed to be paired with clear structure and direction. With graduation in the rearview mirror, she realized their work had to transition from spontaneous acts of rebellion to an organized, enduring initiative.

In one community meeting, Kiera addressed a group of committed citizens. "We've built something powerful here," she began, her voice both soft and resolute. "But our journey doesn't end with high school. The change we've ignited at River Valley must continue, not just for us, but for every person who has ever felt alone or unheard." Her eyes swept over the room, landing on faces that were both determined and vulnerable. "We need to create structures that ensure our voices can reach beyond these corridors — a sustainable network of support, mentorship, and community outreach."

Ideas flowed freely. Someone suggested organizing periodic community forums where students, parents, and local organizations could discuss ongoing challenges and solutions.

Melanie, whose "Voice Circles" evolved into a haven for creative expression, also saw her role expand naturally. The success of the group inspired her to reach out further. She began collaborating with local artists to create community murals celebrating diversity and resilience — public tributes reminding everyone that every individual's story was valuable. In one vibrant workshop held at a community center, Melanie worked alongside peers to design a mural entitled "The Symphony of Voices." Each brushstroke represented a unique story, each color a different emotion, and together, they formed a powerful, collective narrative of hope.

During one of these sessions, Melanie shared her vision with the group. "Imagine a day when our entire community comes together to celebrate our differences — where every piece of art, every poem, every song is a reminder that we are all seen," she said, her eyes sparkling with determination. The idea resonated deeply, and plans developed for "The Festival of Echoes."

In a series of follow-up meetings, Kiera, Evan, Ben, and Melanie collaborated to merge their initiatives into a unified strategy for change. They knew that their movement needed to be more than a high school protest — it had to become an enduring network, one that would continue to advocate for mental health, support vulnerable students, and challenge the systemic issues that had led to Tyler's tragic isolation.

The core group gathered to finalize a comprehensive proposal one crisp afternoon in a conference room lit by soft fluorescent lights. Evan projected the digital archive onto a screen. At the same time, Kiera reviewed the draft document outlining their plans for a long-term peer support program, community workshops, community art murals, and partnerships with local mental health organizations. Every detail was scrutinized and refined. "We're not just asking for change," Kiera said passionately, "we're building it. This proposal is our blueprint for a future where every person feels safe, heard, and valued."

As the meeting progressed, voices mingled in a cacophony of hope and resolve. One lady suggested setting up a dedicated hotline for people in distress. At the same time, another proposed a mentorship program that connected alums with current students — a way to extend the reach of their movement even after graduation. Each idea, no matter how small, was a testament to their collective commitment to ensure that Tyler's legacy was not lost to time.

Late that evening, as the final preparations for a community forum took shape, Kiera reflected for a moment. Standing alone at the edge of a quiet courtyard, she gazed at the stars overhead. In the silence of the night, she thought about Tyler — his gentle smile, calm courage, the small ways attempted to reach out even when he felt utterly alone. That memory, once a source of unbearable regret, now fueled her determination. "We must carry his light forward," she whispered to herself. "Not just as a reminder of our loss, but as a call to action for every soul that has ever felt invisible."

By the time the forum was set to begin the next day, the foundation for lasting change had been laid. The collective plans were ready, the proposal was nearly finalized, and the core group felt unbreakable unity. They knew their journey from grief to action was far from over, but in that moment, they embraced the responsibility of transforming silence into a vibrant chorus of voices.

The Journey Forward – A New Legacy

As the days turned into weeks, the initiatives born out of the forum began to take shape. The digital archive, now rebranded as "The Echoes Project," was launched as an interactive online platform where students and community members could share their personal stories anonymously. The platform quickly became a powerful tool for connection, with hundreds of submissions that recounted experiences of isolation, resilience, and the courage to speak out. Each entry was a testament to the collective healing that took root, a record of the transformative power of vulnerability.

Community engagement began to grow. Local nonprofits and mental health organizations reached out, inspired by the passion and resilience of the students. A community center in a nearby neighbourhood partnered with The Echoes Project to host workshops on emotional well-being and creative expression. The ripple effect was undeniable: a support network that extended well beyond River Valley High was forming, ready to challenge the longstanding culture of silence and neglect.

Melanie continued to lead the "Voice Circles" with quiet determination, her creative spirit now interwoven with a broader vision for the community. Building up to the "Festival of Echoes", she organized a series of public art installations and poetry readings in the town's central park. On the day of one such event, dozens of people gathered under the open sky to share their stories through art, spoken word, and song. A mural, painted collaboratively by local artists and students, depicted a vibrant tapestry of faces and symbols, each representing a unique story of struggle and triumph. As Melanie looked upon the mural, she felt a surge of pride and fulfillment — Tyler's memory was no longer confined to the walls of a high school locker; it had become a living, breathing legacy that belonged to everyone.

Throughout these months of transformation, Evan remained the steadfast chronicler of their journey. His podcast, named after the movement's original inspiration, steadily gained traction. In each episode, he interviewed students, teachers, and community members who shared their experiences and hopes for the future. "Our voices are powerful," he would say at the end of every episode. "They are the threads that weave the fabric of our community. And together, we have the power to mend what was broken."

One evening, as the city park buzzed with the excitement of a new community event, Evan and Kiera sat together on a bench. The night was incredible, and the stars shone brightly overhead — a silent promise of hope for the future. Evan scrolled through the latest messages on The Echoes Project, his eyes alight with the myriad voices that had come together in support. "Look at these," he said, turning the screen toward Kiera. "Every message is a reminder that we're building something real — that even in our darkest moments, there is light."

As the days turned into weeks, the movement grew, intertwining with the lives of everyone in the community. The initiatives launched by the students began to inspire similar efforts in neighboring schools and community centers. The transformation that had started at River Valley High was now a beacon for a broader change — a reminder that when people come together, their collective voice can dismantle even the most entrenched systems of indifference.

Chapter 6: The Next Chapter – Empowering the Future

A New Mission

The dawn broke with a quiet promise that a new day would arise, offering the possibility of renewal and growth. For Evan, Kiera, Ben, and Melanie, the culmination of their high school journey had given birth to a powerful vision: to transform personal loss into a collective force for change that would extend far beyond the familiar corridors of River Valley High.

As the first light of morning filtered through Evan's modest apartment curtains, he sat at his desk with renewed determination. The digital archive, "The Echoes Network," had been a testament to their struggle, a repository of every anonymous confession, every silent cry, every whispered regret that had fueled their movement. Evan began drafting plans for a future project — a traveling exhibit that would carry these stories into the wider community. Every word typed into his document was laced with the memory of Tyler's quiet plea and the promise that no voice, no matter how soft, would ever be allowed to fade into oblivion again.

He had spent long nights coding, designing user-friendly features, and integrating multimedia elements that allowed users to submit stories, photos, and even short video testimonies. Every addition was carefully crafted to ensure the platform was a sanctuary for those in distress and a repository of hope and resilience. Evan knew that this tool had the potential to connect disparate communities, allowing individuals from various backgrounds to share their struggles and triumphs in a safe, moderated environment.

Across town, Kiera awoke with a sense of calm that belied the tumult of her past. Over the past months, the weight of leadership had transformed her from a student burdened by responsibility into a visionary ready to forge a new path. Today, she was not just a former leader of River Valley High, but a beacon for change, determined to empower others to speak out and be heard. Kiera laid the groundwork for a series of public seminars and workshops. Determined to transform her leadership experience into a force for change, she partnered with local community centers and non-profit organizations. She focused on practical, empowering education: teaching skills in active listening, emotional resilience, and peer support. These sessions were designed to help young people navigate their challenges and equip them with the tools to be advocates for one another.

In one of the bustling community centers, Kiera led a seminar titled "The Power of a Listening Heart." The room was filled with participants from diverse backgrounds — teenagers, parents, and even local educators — all eager to learn how to create more inclusive, supportive environments. Kiera's approach was hands-on; she guided the group through role-playing exercises, interactive discussions, and reflective journaling. "True strength," she explained, "comes from the courage to listen, to acknowledge someone's pain, and to stand together in solidarity." The session ended with participants forming small discussion groups, sharing personal experiences, and brainstorming actionable ideas for community improvement.

Ben, whose journey toward self-forgiveness had taken root during his volunteer work at the local community center, was busy planning a mentorship initiative. He had seen firsthand how small acts of kindness could transform lives, and he was determined to extend that support beyond the confines of high school. In one afternoon session at the center, Ben gathered a group of young students who had recently joined the program. Sitting in a circle on a colorful rug, he shared his own story of regret and redemption. "I used to think that staying silent about my feelings kept me safe," he confessed, his voice soft but clear. "But I learned that speaking up — even just to say 'I'm here' — can be the first step in healing." The students listened intently, their eyes reflecting a mix of hope and apprehension. Ben's words resonated with them, igniting a spark that he hoped would grow into a lasting commitment to care for one another.

In a particularly memorable session, Ben sat with a group of seventh-graders in a small, sunlit classroom at the community center. One of the students, a quiet boy named Isaiah, hesitated before speaking. "Sometimes I feel like no matter what I do, I'll never be good enough," Isaiah confessed. Ben leaned in, his tone gentle and sincere. "I understand that feeling, Isaiah. I used to believe that silence was safe, but I've learned that speaking up — even when it's hard — can change everything. You're not alone in this; your story can help someone else feel seen." That simple yet profound conversation ignited a spark in Isaiah, who later approached Ben with a determined smile, saying, "I'm going to try to speak up more." For Ben, moments like these validated the belief that every act of connection was a step toward healing old wounds.

Melanie, whose creative spark had grown into a fierce passion, outlined her vision for "The Festival of Echoes." Her eyes shone as she described a vibrant event merging art, music, and spoken word into a celebration of diversity and resilience. "Our festival will be a call to every person who's ever felt alone," she said. "It will be a platform to share our stories, to transform our pain into beauty, and to remind everyone that every whisper of hope has the power to ignite a revolution." Her vision was poetic and practical, adding another vital layer to the group's plans.

Melanie channeled her passion for creative expression into a series of collaborative art projects that transcended the boundaries of their former school. She coordinated with local artists to host pop-up galleries and street performances celebrating diversity and resilience.

In one vibrant outdoor exhibition held in a busy public park, Melanie's "Voices Unbound" project featured a collection of art pieces contributed by community members, each depicting a personal story of struggle, hope, and the courage to overcome adversity. The event was a sensory tapestry of color and sound, where poetry was recited in spontaneous bursts, and musicians played soulful tunes that resonated deeply with the audience. Melanie's goal was to create a living, breathing tribute to the power of creative expression — a reminder that art could bridge the pain of the past and the promise of the future.

As the initiatives took shape, the team began to see that their projects were not isolated efforts but interconnected components of a more significant movement. They pooled their resources, shared insights, and refined their strategies in a series of joint meetings. A familiar refrain marked their discussions: "Every voice matters." Together, they envisioned a future where the digital platform, the public workshops, the mentorship program, and the art initiatives would work harmoniously to create a robust network of support. Their shared goal was to extend the legacy of their high school movement into a sustainable, community-wide force for change.

Developing the Road Map

One morning, the group gathered at a local co-working space to consolidate their ideas. Evan, Kiera, Ben, and Melanie sat around a large table, the energy, focused and intense, starkly contrasted with the chaos of their earlier high school days.

"We've built something here that is much bigger than any of us," Kiera said, her voice steady and determined. "Our vision must carry forward the promise of every unheard cry and every silent plea. We're not just transforming our community but showing the world that change is possible when we dare to speak up."

Evan added, "The digital platform is our foundation — where all our voices converge. But it's not enough to simply document our stories; we must amplify them. We have plans to launch a series of live events, digital campaigns, and partnerships with local media to ensure that our message reaches far beyond our immediate circle."

He shared his plans for the traveling exhibit. With this immersive experience, digital displays, interactive installations, and personal testimonies would combine to create a living, breathing tribute to the power of collective vulnerability. "Imagine a space where every story is on display, where every anonymous post, every memory, is transformed into art," he explained. "That space would be a reminder that even in our darkest moments, there is hope — and that hope can travel, inspire, and change the world."

The conversation flowed, each idea building on the last. Ben spoke up next, his voice steady as he recounted his experiences at the community center. "I've seen firsthand how a single act of kindness can break through the hardest walls of isolation," he said. "Our mentorship program, for instance, isn't just about tutoring — it's about connecting with someone, letting them know that they matter. I want to expand that, to create a network where older students and community members guide the younger ones, so no one ever feels invisible again." His words were met with nods of agreement, and the room hummed with the sound of collective commitment.

Throughout the meeting, the team crafted a roadmap for their next steps. They planned community outreach events, including the traveling exhibit, local workshops on mental health and creative expression, and public forums to foster dialogue between students, parents, educators, and community leaders. Every suggestion was met with passionate discussion and detailed planning. The conversation flowed effortlessly as they discussed logistics — planning outreach events, scheduling community forums, and mapping out a timeline for rolling out their initiatives.

Their discussion continued late into the night, the plans evolving with each passing hour. Evan began outlining a detailed proposal for a mobile outreach program — a traveling exhibit showcasing The Echoes Project and engaging communities in dialogue about mental health and belonging. Inspired by the artists she met, Melanie drafted plans for public art installations to transform community centers' cold, sterile spaces into vibrant, welcoming environments. She also worked on finalizing the schedule for the "Festival of Echoes". Ben focused on refining the mentorship initiative, ensuring that every young person who joined the program would have a safe space to express themselves. Kiera drafted letters to community leaders, interested businesses, non-profits and other stakeholders seeking assistance and funding to expand their ideas.

As the night deepened, the co-working space emptied, but the energy of that meeting lingered. Over the following days, plans were set in motion. The digital platform, now rebranded as "The Echoes Network," was scheduled for its public launch; community forums were being organized in various neighborhoods; and preparations for the Festival of Echoes were underway. Each project was a thread in the intricate tapestry of their shared vision — a tapestry that promised to transform personal pain into a beacon of collective hope.

Building Bridges Beyond the Campus

On a bright morning, Evan met with a small group of local youth leaders at the town's community center. Modest and warmly lit, the room buzzed with the low conversation hum and the occasional clatter of coffee cups. Evan laid out his vision on a whiteboard, his handwriting both hurried and determined. "We need to take these stories into the community," he explained. "Our archive isn't just about what happened at River Valley — it's a mirror for every town and school where people feel isolated. Imagine an exhibit that travels from one neighborhood to another, sparking conversations and inspiring action."

The local leaders listened intently, their faces reflecting curiosity and cautious optimism. One of them, a community organizer named Lisa, nodded slowly. "I've seen too many kids struggle in silence," she said. "If your project can help them feel seen and heard, it's worth pursuing. We can help you set up meetings with local schools and public spaces."

Evan's eyes lit up. "That's exactly what we need — a bridge between our voices and the broader community."

One afternoon, while organizing a workshop on creative expression, Kiera met Marcus — a high school senior from a neighboring district who had struggled with feelings of isolation due to cultural differences. Over cups of herbal tea, they discussed the challenges of feeling like an outsider in a world that prized conformity. "I used to think that if I blended in, no one would notice my struggles," Marcus confessed. "But now I see that by hiding, I only made it harder for people to reach out." Kiera nodded in understanding, sharing her journey of coming to terms with the burden of leadership. "It's about finding balance," she said softly. "We need to trust others to carry the weight too."

Inspired by these conversations, Kiera began to organize community art projects that invited young people from diverse backgrounds to contribute. One project, in particular, involved creating a large mosaic that represented the many voices of the community. Each tile was to be painted by a student, depicting a word or symbol that resonated with their story. The project celebrated individuality and built bridges between different cultures and neighborhoods. As the mosaic took shape on the wall of the community center, it became a living testament to the idea that every person's voice was a vital part of a larger, interconnected tapestry.

Ben, too, was busy stepping into new roles. His journey of self-forgiveness had taught him that the path to healing was often found in helping others. Ben's experience volunteering at a community center had opened his eyes to the struggles faced by many local children — struggles that echoed his past regrets. He initiated a mentorship program in partnership with the center, pairing older students with younger ones who needed guidance. In one memorable session, Ben sat with a group of freshmen in a sunlit room. With gentle patience, he recounted his own story of guilt and transformation. "I didn't realize that my words could hurt others," he admitted. "Instead of putting others down, we need to lift them up. I'm here for you, and I hope one day you'll be here for someone else, too." Once etched with apprehension, the faces of the young students gradually brightened with hope. Ben realized that by helping others, he was also piecing together his broken past — turning regret into a steppingstone for change.

Across town, Melanie's creative spirit was evolving into a powerful tool for community engagement. The success of her artistic endeavors inspired her to envision an even larger platform — a traveling festival that would celebrate art, music, and poetry as vehicles for healing and expression. Over a series of late-night planning sessions in local cafés, Melanie and a group of like-minded community members drafted plans for "The Festival of Echoes." They envisioned a day when local artists, poets, and musicians would come together to share their stories, turning personal pain into public art. "We can use our creativity to remind everyone that even in the darkest moments, beauty and hope can emerge," Melanie declared during one animated discussion. The idea resonated deeply, and soon, word spread throughout the community. Local galleries, small theaters, and even a city park expressed interest in hosting parts of the festival.

They began coordinating with local media, drafting press releases about their journey from silent despair to collective action. Evan's podcast, which started as a chronicle of grief, was being rebranded to include interviews with community members, teachers, and local leaders who shared their struggles with isolation and the power of coming together.

In one pivotal meeting at the community center, the group gathered around a large table, their laptops open and minds buzzing with ideas. The room, once a quiet space for solitary study, now thrummed with the energy of collaboration. "Our story isn't just about what happened at River Valley," Kiera said, addressing the group passionately. "It's about every community that has ever let silence win. We have the power to change that narrative. We can create a network of support that reaches far beyond our school — a movement that shows every person that they are seen and valued."

The discussion turned to logistics: securing a venue for the festival, partnering with local nonprofits, and planning workshops on mental health and creative expression. Each idea was a thread in the tapestry they were weaving — a tapestry that promised to bridge the gap between the isolated voices of the past and the united chorus of the future.

"We've seen what happens when we let silence rule," Kiera said. "Now it's time to build bridges of understanding and compassion that extend to every corner of our community."

With every plan made and every idea discussed, the movement gained momentum. The digital platform — now called "The Echoes Network" — was set to launch publicly within weeks, offering a space where anyone could share their story anonymously, receive support, or simply read the words of others who had once felt alone. The community partnerships, once just a hopeful dream, became concrete plans with scheduled workshops, art installations, and public forums.

That evening, as the group dispersed and the city settled into a peaceful twilight, the sense of possibility was palpable. Evan sat alone on a bench outside the community center, his mind full of the day's events. He scrolled through his notes, each a testament to the resilience of the human spirit and a reminder of Tyler's enduring legacy. "This is just the beginning," he whispered, his voice resolute. "Our voices are rising, and soon, they'll echo across every street, every neighborhood."

In a small apartment across town, Kiera prepared for a late-night video call with a local nonprofit leader eager to collaborate on the upcoming festival. As she arranged her notes and rehearsed her presentation, she couldn't help but feel that the transformation they were building was not just for themselves but for everyone who had ever felt unseen or unheard. "Tyler's memory will guide us," she said softly, "and our shared courage will light the way forward."

At that moment, the weight of the past and the promise of the future merged into a powerful vision — a community united by empathy, resilience, and the unyielding belief that every silent cry must be heard. The movement was no longer a reaction to tragedy but a proactive, living force — a network of voices ready to break the chains of indifference and build a future defined by connection and hope.

As the night deepened and the city lights flickered on one by one, Evan, Kiera, Ben, and Melanie knew they were on the cusp of something truly transformative. The bridges they were building would extend far beyond the walls of their old school, reaching into every heart that had ever been left alone. With every step forward, they were crafting a new legacy where every whisper, cry, and hopeful voice contributed to a tapestry of lasting change.

And so, with the stars as their witness and the echoes of their past guiding their every move, they stepped boldly into the new day, ready to share their voices with a world waiting to listen.

Venturing into the Wider World

With the "Festival of Echoes" now a concrete plan, Melanie coordinated with local art galleries, coffee shops, and a small theater to host mini events showcasing poetry readings, art installations, and acoustic performances. Melanie stood before a small but attentive crowd on the day of one such event in the town square. The sky was clear, and gentle breezes rustled the leaves of nearby trees.

"This festival is about celebrating every voice — especially those that have been silenced for too long," she declared. "Our art, stories, and music are a testament to our resilience. We create a symphony of hope that can overcome any darkness." The crowd responded with quiet applause, and as a local musician strummed a soulful melody on his guitar, the energy in the square shifted from quiet sorrow to the promise of shared healing.

The various efforts merged into a cohesive network at the community center. Evan and Kiera organized a joint meeting with representatives from the local youth organization, community leaders, and educators. In a large, sunlit room, they presented "The Echoes Project" as a model for community engagement. This initiative had started as a high school movement but was ready to be adapted to the broader community's needs. Screens displayed the digital archive, and live testimonies from students filled the room with raw emotion. "These are not just stories," Evan emphasized, "they are the voices of every person who has ever felt ignored. They are the building blocks of a community where no cry for help goes unanswered."

The discussions were animated and sometimes heated as the group grappled with the challenges of replicating a grassroots effort in a larger, more diverse environment. There were concerns about funding, cultural differences, and the scale of change needed. Yet, every challenge was met with a determined spirit. Kiera's insistence that change must start with genuine connection and empathy resonated with everyone in the room. "It doesn't matter how big the system is," she said firmly. "If we can reach one person and make a small difference in one's life, that's a victory. And together, those victories will add up."

Evan found himself energized by the commitment of the local leaders. As the meeting drew to a close, a consensus emerged — a plan to launch a pilot outreach program that would include a traveling exhibit, community forums, and regular workshops on mental health and creative expression. "We're not just taking our voices beyond the halls," Evan declared as he closed his laptop. "We're taking them to every corner of this community, ensuring that every person who has ever felt isolated is given the chance to be heard."

That evening, as the new initiatives began to take shape, the group gathered on the steps of the community center. The sky was a deep indigo, scattered with stars that seemed to watch over them. Evan, Kiera, Ben, and Melanie stood side by side, their faces illuminated by the soft glow of streetlights and the quiet satisfaction.

"I'm both excited and terrified," Kiera confessed, her voice barely audible over the gentle night breeze. "We're stepping into uncharted territory — where the stakes are higher and the challenges even greater. But I believe that if we hold onto what we've learned here and remember that every voice matters, we can make a real difference."

The promise of the new horizon was not just an abstract idea — it was a tangible, living reality. The community began to understand that change was possible when individuals came together, when personal pain was transformed into collective strength, and when every voice, no matter how quiet, was allowed to be heard.

Each group member carried a renewed sense of purpose as they dispersed into the cool night. The pilot programs launched, and the digital platform live, connected the project with communities far beyond River Valley High. Every step they took was toward a future where isolation was replaced by inclusion and silence by the powerful sound of collective hope.

Standing at the edge of the community center's parking lot, Evan paused and looked back at the building that had been their launching pad. The campus of River Valley High, now a cherished chapter in their journey, had given them the courage to face the wider world. With that courage, they were ready to build bridges, break down barriers, and ensure that no one ever faced their struggles alone.

Forging New Alliances

Melanie made great strides in her creative endeavors. She arranged for a local art gallery to host a preliminary exhibit featuring work from the "Festival of Echoes". The exhibit, "Voices of Hope," showcased paintings, sculptures, and mixed media art created by students and local artists. Every piece was a tribute to the struggle against silence — a celebration of the unique stories that had once been confined to hidden corners. At the opening reception, Melanie spoke passionately about the importance of art as a vehicle for change. "Every brushstroke, every line, is a declaration that our stories matter," she said. "This exhibit is not just about mourning what was lost — celebrating our resilience and building a future where every voice can shine."

As these initiatives began to take root, the impact of their efforts became visible throughout the community. Local newspapers ran articles on "The Echoes Network," highlighting the innovative projects and the collaborative spirit driving them forward. Teachers in neighboring schools reported that similar student-led support groups were emerging, inspired by the movement at River Valley High. Once resistant to change, even the administration started to engage with the new programs, offering limited support and promising a further review of school policies regarding mental health and inclusion.

That evening, as the sun set over the town, casting a golden glow over the community center, the steering committee gathered for a final planning session. In the soft light of the meeting room, the group pored over the proposals, revised timelines, and feedback from the first outreach events. The atmosphere was one of cautious optimism tempered by the hard lessons of the past. Evan summarized their progress: "We've built a foundation — a network that reaches from our old halls into the heart of this community. We have the stories, we have the passion, and now we have the plan to make lasting change."

Kiera's eyes, reflecting determination and a hint of weariness, added, "Our next step is to launch these programs officially. The pilot outreach will start next month, and by then, we need to have every detail in place — from the traveling exhibit to the mentorship programs and the community art projects. Tyler's memory is our guide, and we owe it to him and every unheard cry to make sure our voices are heard and lead to real, systemic change."

As the meeting concluded, the weight of their mission settled over the group — a promise that the pain of the past would be transformed into the power of the future. Stepping out into the cool night air, Kiera and Evan stood together on the steps outside the community center. They gazed at a sky strewn with stars, each a tiny beacon of hope. "We're ready," Evan murmured, "to carry this movement forward — to build bridges connecting every isolated voice with a community that cares."

With that, the group dispersed into the night, each person carrying the promise of a better tomorrow. The digital platform, "The Echoes Network," was set to launch publicly soon, and plans for community forums and art installations moved steadily forward. In every step, every shared idea, and every quiet act of kindness, the seeds of transformation were being sown — seeds that would, over time, grow into a powerful movement of connection, empathy, and hope.

Chapter 7: Empowering the Future

Empowering Others Through Shared Vision

In a subsequent meeting at a local cultural center, the team convened with representatives from several neighborhood organizations — nonprofits, art collectives, and mental health advocates. The atmosphere in the room was one of mutual respect and shared purpose. Kiera led the discussion with a clear message: "Our goal is to create a network where every individual feels seen, heard, and valued. We're not here just to document our pain but to transform it into a force that uplifts everyone."

One community leader, Ms. Rivera, spoke passionately about the importance of cultural sensitivity. "In our city, many feel isolated not only because of personal struggles but also because they don't see their own stories reflected in the mainstream," she explained. "Your movement, focusing on real, raw experiences, can change that narrative." Her words resonated with the group, reinforcing the need for an inclusive approach that embraced all voices, regardless of background or circumstance.

During this meeting, the team also discussed the logistics of "The Festival of Echoes," an upcoming event to celebrate these new alliances. Melanie presented a detailed plan for the festival, including art exhibitions, poetry slams, live music, and interactive workshops. "This festival will be more than just a celebration — it will be a public declaration that every story matters," she said. The proposal was met with enthusiastic support, and soon, a subcommittee was formed to handle the festival's organization.

Ben reviewed a list of potential mentors and community partners in a quiet corner of the meeting room. He focused on ensuring the mentorship network was robust enough to provide sustained support. "We're not just here to offer a temporary fix," he said. "We need to build a system that continues to support young people long after our initial efforts. That means training, resources, and a genuine commitment to making change permanent." His words underscored the shift from a reactive movement to a proactive, ongoing mission.

Forging Partnerships for Lasting Impact

The following week, the group held one-on-one meetings with key community stakeholders. Evan met with a local radio station manager to discuss launching a series of live call-in shows where community members could share their stories in real-time. Kiera sat down with educators from nearby schools to plan joint workshops, ensuring that the momentum from their movement could be replicated in other institutions. Ben connected with leaders at various after-school programs, advocating for a mentorship curriculum to benefit a broader range of students. Meanwhile, Melanie collaborated with a local art director to curate an exhibition that would travel between community centers and public spaces.

Each meeting reinforced one central idea: the power of collective action. Every partnership formed was a step toward building a network of care that extended far beyond their own experiences at River Valley High. The team was not just charting a path for themselves — they were creating avenues for everyone in the community to feel empowered and connected.

The group reconvened for a final strategy session at the innovation hub. The room was filled with tangible plans — detailed timelines, budget proposals, and creative mock-ups of the upcoming initiatives. Evan clicked through slides on his laptop, each illustrating a different aspect of their vision. "Our goal," he explained, "is to make sure that every person who feels alone can access the support they need — whether through a digital platform, a mentorship session, or a community art project."

Kiera leaned forward, her eyes bright with determination. "This is our legacy," she said softly. "We began with the pain of a lost friend, but now we're building a future where every voice is heard, and every story is valued. Our work here empowers us and every individual who has ever felt unseen."

Their collective energy was palpable as they finalized their roadmap for the coming months. The plan was ambitious, but each step was carefully designed to build on past successes while addressing the challenges of scaling their movement. With every partnership forged and every new initiative planned, the promise of a brighter future grew stronger.

Sustaining the Vision

As the months passed after the initial surge of transformative energy, Evan, Kiera, Ben, and Melanie faced a new challenge: how to sustain the vision that had taken root during their high school years and ensure its impact would be lasting. Their journey from personal grief to collective action had laid a robust foundation — but they now understood that actual change required careful nurturing, long-term planning, and an unwavering commitment to the values they had embraced.

The group reconvened in a renovated community meeting space on a cool, overcast morning. The walls, once bare, were now adorned with inspirational quotes and vibrant murals — a living testament to the movement's evolution. Around a large oval table, the team gathered with a mix of familiar faces and new partners: representatives from local non-profits, educators, and community leaders drawn by the promise of "The Echoes Network." The room's energy was hopeful and determined, as everyone recognized that sustaining a movement was a marathon, not a sprint.

Evan opened the meeting by projecting an updated version of "The

Echoes Network" on a large screen. "We've reached an important milestone," he said, his voice steady and confident. "Our digital platform now hosts over a thousand stories — each a testament to the struggles and resilience of our community. But numbers alone aren't enough. We need to ensure that this platform evolves, remains a safe space for voices to be heard, and serves as a bridge to real-world action."

Kiera leaned forward, her eyes alight with purpose. "Our next phase is about sustainability," she explained. "We must develop protocols, secure funding, and create partnerships that will allow our initiatives to thrive. This means formalizing our mentorship programs, expanding our community workshops, and integrating our online platform with local services."

A detailed discussion ensued as the group mapped out a strategic plan. They broke down their goals into actionable steps: establishing a mentorship board, applying for local grants, setting up regular training sessions for peer leaders, and launching a series of pilot workshops in nearby neighborhoods. Each idea was scrutinized and refined, ensuring that the movement's core values — compassion, inclusion, and empowerment — remained at the forefront.

One community partner, Ms. Rivera from a local youth advocacy organization, spoke passionately about the importance of continuity. "Too often, movements begin with a burst of energy and then fade away," she noted. "What you are building here is a model for sustained change. We can help by providing resources, mentoring your leadership team, and integrating your programs with our community services. The key is to ensure that every initiative is backed by real support and that there's a structure in place to adapt and grow."

As the meeting progressed, Melanie presented a refined proposal for "The Festival of Echoes." Her presentation was a vibrant collage of images, testimonials, and projected timelines. "The festival will serve not only as an annual celebration of our movement but as a recurring reminder to our community that art, creativity, and shared stories are powerful tools for healing," she declared. "We're planning interactive installations, live performances, and open mic sessions that invite everyone to participate and share their journey. This isn't just about commemorating the past — it's about inspiring a continuous dialogue that reaches every corner of our community."

Evan then detailed his vision for the enhanced digital platform. "We plan to introduce a live chat feature moderated by trained peer counselors, integrate local mental health resources, and offer webinars with experts on topics ranging from emotional resilience to creative expression. The platform will be more than an archive — an active hub for support and engagement." His eyes shone with technical determination and personal passion, underscoring how deeply this project had come to mean for him.

Throughout the meeting, the atmosphere was charged with a sense of continuity. It was clear that the movement was maturing into a robust network that would extend beyond the transient energy of youth and become a lasting institution in the community. Every participant recognized that their work was now about creating a legacy. In this future, every silent cry, every whispered regret, would be transformed into a beacon of support and empowerment.

After the formal session ended, the group lingered in the meeting space, discussing personal visions for the future. In a quiet corner, Evan and Kiera reflected on the journey that had brought them to this point. "I remember when all we had were whispered messages on RiverChat," Evan mused. "Now, we're planning community forums, digital resources, and public art projects. It's amazing how much can happen when people refuse to be silenced."

Kiera nodded thoughtfully. "It wasn't just about overcoming our past — building something new. Something that would ensure that no one ever feels invisible again. And that's what sustains me: the belief that every small act of kindness, every connection we make, will add up to a future where every voice is heard."

The future was uncertain, and challenges lay ahead, but with every plan executed, every partnership forged, and every voice uplifted, the vision of a connected, compassionate community became increasingly tangible. The group's dedication to transforming silence into support was a beacon of hope for everyone who had ever felt unseen.

A Legacy Unfolding: The Future Realized

The day's soft light broke over the city with the promise of a new beginning — a beginning forged from the trials, triumphs, and transformative experiences of the past months. For Evan, Kiera, Ben, and Melanie, the journey they had embarked upon at River Valley High had evolved into something far greater than any one of them could imagine. Their movement, once a reaction to a painful loss, matured into a legacy of empowerment, unity, and enduring change. Now, as they gathered to reflect on their collective achievements and chart the path forward, a sense of fulfillment mixed with anticipation filled the air.

In a quiet, renovated hall of a local community center — the same space where many of their early meetings had taken place — the four friends, community leaders, and a select group of student leaders convened for one final review of their progress. The room, bathed in the soft glow of evening light filtering through large windows, buzzed with reflective energy. On one wall, a timeline of events was meticulously displayed: the early days of whispered grief, the formation of "The Whisperers," the creation of "The Echoes Project," and the series of community forums and public art events that had spread their message beyond the confines of their former school.

Evan opened the meeting by scrolling through the digital archive on his laptop. "When we started, our platform was just a repository of anonymous posts and memories," he began, his tone measured and proud. "Now, it's a living network that documents our past and serves as a springboard for future projects. Every story and voice captured here is proof that our movement has grown — and will continue to grow."

Kiera, seated beside him, nodded in agreement. "We've transformed our pain into a movement that empowers others. Our work isn't finished, but today is a moment to celebrate how far we've come. Look at the turnout at our forums, the positive feedback from the workshops, and the art installations that have sparked new conversations across the community." She paused, her eyes reflecting both nostalgia and hope. "Tyler's memory was the spark, but our legacy is now something we all share."

Across the table, Ben reflected on his role as a mentor. "I remember when I first felt overwhelmed by guilt — believing my words hurt Tyler. But each day, by connecting with younger students and offering support, I've learned that our voices can heal even the deepest wounds. Our mentorship program now has dozens of active pairings, and every success story clarifies that our collective effort is making a difference."

Melanie added, "Art has been our universal language. The art installations, our public murals, and the collaborative exhibitions honor our past and give us a vision for the future. We're telling the world that even in our darkest moments, beauty and hope can be found." Her voice carried a quiet passion, and images of colorful murals and vibrant performances danced in everyone's mind as she spoke.

With the progress laid out before them, the group began discussing the next steps. They recognized that sustaining their movement would require robust support structures, clear goals, and ongoing community engagement. Evan proposed that they form an advisory board composed of both former students and local community leaders, ensuring that the projects could adapt and evolve. "This board would oversee the digital platform, guide the mentorship program, and help secure funding for future initiatives," he explained. "It's about building a legacy that will outlast us."

Kiera was quick to support the idea. "We need to institutionalize our efforts. Our workshops and forums have been successful because they're built on genuine connections. Formalizing this process will allow us to reach even more people and create sustainable change." She suggested regular review sessions, where the advisory board could gather participant feedback and adjust their programs accordingly. "Continuous improvement is key," she said, "so every cry for help can be met with the best support possible."

Ben shared his vision for expanding the mentorship program. "Imagine if every high school and middle school in our district had access to a network of trained mentors — people who know what it's like to struggle in silence and have the courage to speak up. I want to see our program replicated in other communities so that our experience can help break the cycle of isolation on a much larger scale." His words resonated with the group, and plans were quickly drawn up to reach neighboring schools and community centers.

Melanie's final point was a call for creative expression to remain at the heart of their movement. "Our art projects, festivals, and exhibitions have been instrumental in giving voice to our journey. We should establish an annual event that celebrates stories and creativity that brings together students, artists, and community members. This event will serve as a memorial to Tyler and celebrate our shared resilience." The idea was agreed enthusiastically, and Melanie volunteered to spearhead the planning.

The sense of accomplishment was palpable as the meeting drew to a close. The group knew that while their movement had already transformed many lives, the work was far from over. They spent a few more minutes discussing minor details, refining the timelines, and assigning responsibilities for the advisory board and outreach initiatives.

The cool evening air greeted them outside the meeting room as they stepped out together. Evan paused momentarily, looking up at the starry sky, feeling the weight of their shared journey and the promise of the future. "Every voice matters," he whispered. "And now, our legacy is built not just on what we endured, but on what we're creating together."

Kiera smiled, her eyes soft with both gratitude and determination. "We're paving the way for a future where no one has to feel invisible. Tyler's silence sparked this movement, but our voices will carry it forward into a world where every cry is met with empathy, and every hope is given a chance to shine."

Standing beside them, Ben added quietly, "I used to feel that my past mistakes would forever define me. But now, every time I see a young person find the courage to speak up, I know that our shared journey can heal more than just our wounds — it can heal an entire community."

Melanie's voice joined the quiet chorus, "And art will always remind us that even in the hardest moments, beauty and hope are never truly lost. Our creativity is our strength — the language unites us all."

In the following days and weeks, the initiatives discussed in that meeting took shape. The advisory board was formed, bringing together a diverse group committed to mental health and community support. Mentorship programs expanded into a network that reached multiple schools, and the digital platform, "The Echoes Network," became a hub for stories, resources, and ongoing dialogue. Inspired by Melanie's vision, the annual festival was set for the following year — a celebration of art, music, and the enduring power of community.

Chapter 8: Reaching Beyond — A Global Vision

New Beginnings and Global Aspirations

The soft glow of dawn revealed a world transformed by possibility. For Evan, Kiera, Ben, and Melanie, the journey within the familiar halls of River Valley High had evolved into a vision that stretched far beyond local borders. Now, as they prepared to step into a wider arena, every lesson learned from Tyler's silence, every act of courage that had blossomed into a movement, resonated like a beacon of hope. This was when their shared struggle and triumph were ready to inspire a broader change — a global vision built on empathy, connection, and unwavering resolve.

Evan awoke early in his modest apartment, the remnants of his high school days mingling with the excitement of the future. He sat at his desk, the digital archive of "The Echoes Network" still open on his computer. Unlike before — when the archive was a solitary repository of anonymous cries — the platform now represented a community of voices. Each post and story had the power to spark dialogue and foster understanding. But as he scrolled through the entries, his thoughts naturally drifted beyond the familiar streets of River Valley. "What if these stories could reach every corner of the globe?" he wondered aloud. At that moment, a seed of a new idea began to form: a traveling, interactive exhibit that would not only showcase his community's raw emotions and transformative experiences but also invite others worldwide to share their tales of struggle and resilience.

Kiera felt a similar stirring. Her journey through the pain and the collective healing at River Valley had changed her profoundly. No longer was her purpose confined to organizing workshops or facilitating "Voice Circles"; now, she dreamed of creating a global platform — a movement that would bring together diverse communities to learn from one another's experiences. That morning, as she sipped her tea in the quiet of her kitchen, she opened her journal and began sketching ideas for a series of international forums on mental health and empowerment. "We have a story that can unite people from every culture," she wrote. "If we share our message of hope, every whisper of despair can become a global chorus for change." Her pen moved swiftly, capturing the vision of connecting small communities with more extensive networks of support, transcending language, borders, and cultural differences.

Ben, whose own transformation had been fueled by mentorship and personal accountability, was also busy preparing for his next step. He recalled the many evenings spent at the community center, the moments of quiet connection with younger students who felt invisible. Those experiences had taught him that every one-on-one conversation had the potential to heal and inspire. Now, he envisioned expanding the mentorship program into a network that reached out to schools and youth centers in their city and neighboring regions — and eventually, globally. "Imagine a network of mentors across different countries," he mused as he organized his notes one crisp morning. "If we can share our strategies and successes, we might create a ripple effect that transforms lives far beyond what we've already achieved." His heart, filled with the burden of past regrets and the excitement of new beginnings, he began drafting a proposal for an international mentorship initiative.

Meanwhile, Melanie's creative spirit was alight with possibilities. The Festival of Echoes, which had grown into a vibrant celebration of art and resilience at the local level, now seemed like only the first step in a much grander vision. In her small studio, surrounded by canvases and art supplies, she worked feverishly on a new project that would merge visual art, music, and spoken word from communities worldwide. "Art transcends borders," she often reminded herself. "Our stories, our emotions — they are universal." Melanie envisioned a series of popup art exhibitions that would travel internationally, each one themed around the idea that creativity can be the spark that lights the way even in the darkest moments. She began contacting fellow artists on social media drafting emails and proposals to art collectives in various countries. Her excitement was palpable as she imagined diverse voices coming together to create a tapestry of shared human experience.

As the day unfolded, the four friends found themselves in a video conference — a new ritual they had adopted to keep their vision aligned despite the physical distances that were beginning to separate them. The screen flickered to life, and their familiar faces appeared side by side, each carrying the unmistakable glow of determination.

Evan opened the conversation. "We've achieved so much locally," he said, "but our work doesn't have to stop here. What if we took our movement global? I'm talking about connecting with other communities that face similar struggles, creating platforms for sharing stories, and amplifying every voice that has been silenced."

Kiera's eyes shone with resolve. "I agree. I've been sketching ideas for international forums — where people can come together, share their challenges, and learn from each other. It could be a powerful way to build empathy on a global scale."

Ben added, "And imagine if our mentorship model could be

replicated in different parts of the world. It doesn't have to be the same, but the core idea — supporting young people so they never feel alone — could resonate everywhere."

Melanie nodded. "Art has always been a universal language. I want to see our Festival of Echoes evolve into a traveling celebration of creativity and resilience. We could showcase stories from every corner of the globe, proving that even amid pain, beauty can emerge."

The conversation flowed easily and belied the enormity of their new ambitions. They discussed logistics, potential partners, funding strategies, and the challenges of scaling their initiatives internationally. Evan spoke about leveraging digital media and social platforms to reach a global audience, while Kiera emphasized the importance of cultural sensitivity and local adaptation. Ben highlighted the need for robust training programs for mentors in different communities, and Melanie shared her ideas for collaborative art projects that would honor diverse cultural expressions.

As the meeting continued, the vision for a global movement began to crystallize. They agreed on the first step: to pilot a series of virtual forums where people from different regions could join in, share their experiences, and collaborate on solutions. Evan volunteered to coordinate with tech-savvy members of their network to create an online interface for these forums. This space could facilitate live discussions, workshops, and resource-sharing across borders.

Kiera proposed they start by contacting a few international organizations focused on youth mental health and empowerment. "We need partners who understand that while our experiences at River Valley are unique, the struggles we face are universal," she explained. "By collaborating with established organizations, we can learn from their expertise and expand our impact."

Ben and Melanie were tasked with drafting initial proposals for their respective programs, ensuring that the core values of empathy, connection, and resilience were at the heart of every initiative. Their goal was to create documents that outlined their plans and conveyed the raw emotion and urgency that had driven their movement from its inception.

The team took intermittent breaks throughout the day to reflect on their progress. In one such moment, Evan stepped away from his computer to walk outside. As he strolled along the quiet city streets, he felt the cool breeze and watched the early morning light reflect off building windows. He thought of Tyler — not just as a memory of loss but as the catalyst that had sparked their entire journey. "Tyler's silence is no longer a void — it's the seed of a global conversation," he whispered to himself, feeling both the weight of responsibility and the thrill of possibility.

Meanwhile, Kiera found herself at a local café, reviewing notes on her tablet. Surrounded by the soft murmur of conversation and the aroma of freshly brewed coffee, she allowed herself a moment of quiet introspection. The path ahead was filled with uncertainties, but the collective determination she felt made every risk seem worth it. "We're not just building programs," she thought, "we're building bridges that connect hearts worldwide."

By late afternoon, the group reconvened for a final video call. The screen displayed their tired but determined faces, each reflecting the passion of their shared vision. Evan summarized their plan, "We're launching the virtual forums next month. I'll work with our tech team to ensure the platform is ready. Kiera, you'll contact international partners. Ben and Melanie, refine your proposals for the mentorship network and the traveling festival. Let's ensure that every voice is given a space to be heard, no matter where it comes from."

Their conversation ended on a note of united purpose. As they signed off, each member felt a renewed sense of possibility — a belief that their movement could transcend geographical boundaries and touch lives far beyond their community.

As the world outside settled into a slumber that night, Evan sat at his desk and began drafting a message for "The Echoes Network." It was a call to action — a message meant to inspire their immediate community and anyone, anywhere, who had ever felt isolated. "We are the voices of hope," he typed, "and we are ready to listen, share, and build a future where every cry for help is transformed into a celebration of life." He saved the draft with a deep commitment, knowing this was only the beginning of their global journey.

In this new phase, every step was a deliberate act of connection. The digital platform would soon become a vibrant hub of international dialogue, the virtual forums a space where cultural differences were not barriers but opportunities for learning and growth, and the community partnerships a network that could extend their message of empathy to all corners of the globe. Each initiative was carefully designed to ensure that their core values — compassion, resilience, and inclusivity — remained at the forefront.

As dawn approached the next day, Evan, Kiera, Ben, and Melanie each prepared for the challenges ahead. They were no longer just the survivors of a tragic loss; they had become ambassadors for change — a generation determined to ensure that no voice would ever be left unheard. Their mission was clear, and their resolve was unyielding: to transform personal pain into a global connection force and empower every individual to believe that their story mattered.

Stepping out into the early light, they felt a surge of optimism. The world was vast, and the challenges were many, but together, they carried Tyler's legacy. This legacy would remind them that the slightest whisper could spark a revolution, even in the most profound silence.

As the group looked toward a horizon filled with promise, the vision of a connected, compassionate global community shone brightly in that moment. They were ready to take their movement to the next level, knowing that every story shared would add to the symphony of hope they were determined to create. The journey ahead was uncertain, but the bonds they had forged, and the lessons they had learned would guide them as they set out to chart new paths and build bridges beyond the walls of their past.

Global Connections: Building International Bridges

The momentum of new beginnings was not confined to the borders of a single town — it was a call that echoed far beyond, inviting communities from different cultures, languages, and backgrounds to join a shared movement for change. With the vision of a global impact taking shape, Evan, Kiera, Ben, and Melanie turned their attention to building bridges across borders, determined to extend the transformative power of "The Echoes Network" and their collective initiatives to an international audience.

In the weeks following the launch of their digital platform, Evan received an unexpected email from a youth organization in Europe. The message was brief but powerful: "We have long faced the same silence in our schools. We want to learn more about your journey." Evan's heart raced as he read the email, realizing their movement resonated far beyond River Valley High. He quickly arranged a video conference, and soon, a virtual meeting was set with representatives from several international organizations dedicated to youth empowerment and mental health advocacy.

During the video call, voices in different accents filled the screen — young leaders and experienced advocates from countries as diverse as Spain, India, and Brazil. They shared their experiences, revealing that the struggles of isolation, silent suffering, and systemic neglect were universal. One representative from Spain, Lucia, said, "In our country, many students feel the pressure to conform. Your digital archive and approach to open dialogue gives us hope that we, too, can break the cycle of silence." The discussion was warm, inclusive, and full of promise. Evan took detailed notes, brainstorming ways to adapt "The Echoes Network" to cater to multiple languages and cultural contexts.

Meanwhile, Kiera was busy coordinating with local cultural centers and embassies to set up international forums to serve as safe spaces for sharing stories across borders. At a community center in her city, she met with a cultural attaché from the local consulate, who expressed enthusiasm for the project. "Our community here is a tapestry of different nationalities and traditions," the attaché remarked. "A forum that brings together these diverse voices could serve as a model for inclusivity and empathy on a global scale." Kiera's mind raced with possibilities — she envisioned a series of annual international forums where participants could exchange ideas, discuss mental health challenges, and celebrate the strength of diverse voices. She promised to draft a proposal outlining the format, potential venues, and collaborative strategies.

Ben, whose mentorship program had already expanded locally, saw an opportunity to extend his reach beyond regional borders. Inspired by the idea of creating a network of mentors that spanned countries, he started researching successful mentorship models worldwide. He contacted former teachers and counselors with experience with international youth programs and began outlining a pilot initiative to pair mentors and mentees across countries.

"Imagine a program where a student from a rural area in Brazil could connect with a mentor in our city," Ben mused during one brainstorming session with his colleagues. "Their shared experiences of feeling isolated might build a bridge that transcends language and distance." Determined to make this idea a reality, Ben drafted an initial proposal and contacted several international organizations for input and potential collaboration.

At the same time, Melanie's creative vision for the "Festival of Echoes" was rapidly evolving. The local success of her public art installations had drawn the attention of artists from abroad. An acclaimed muralist from South Africa responded to one of her social media posts, sharing his admiration for the movement and expressing interest in a collaborative project. Melanie was thrilled. She organized a series of virtual workshops with artists from different countries, discussing techniques, cultural influences, and the universal language of art as a tool for healing.

"Art has the power to unite us even when words fail," she told the group during one animated session. "Our stories, regardless of where they originate, share the same underlying themes of pain, resilience, and hope." These virtual workshops not only enriched her vision but also led to the creation of a joint international art project — a traveling mural that would be installed in various cities, each section reflecting the unique stories and cultural heritage of its location.

As the weeks passed, the group's international outreach began to materialize into tangible projects. Evan worked tirelessly to integrate multilingual support into "The Echoes Network." He collaborated with volunteer translators and tech experts to create an interface that allowed users worldwide to submit their stories in their native languages, ensuring that the platform was accessible and inclusive. With each new story added, the platform became richer — a mosaic of voices that spanned continents and cultures.

Kiera, in parallel, finalized plans for an international forum scheduled for the following summer. The forum would rotate between cities, allowing local communities to host and share their experiences while learning from others. Her proposal included interactive sessions, panel discussions with mental health experts, and creative breakout groups where participants could collaborate on art projects. "We want this forum to be a haven for voices that have been silenced," she explained during a planning session. "It's not just an event — it's the start of a global conversation about how we can build communities that truly care."

Ben's international mentorship initiative was gaining traction as well. He had managed to secure preliminary interest from schools in neighboring regions. Now, he was setting up a pilot program connecting mentors and mentees across different countries via video conferencing. During one test session, he paired a mentor from his hometown with a young student from a rural district in a neighboring country. The session was filled with awkward silences, but the connection grew stronger as they shared their experiences. "I feel like I can finally talk about what's been holding me back," the student confessed through a shaky video call. The mentor, with gentle patience, assured him that his voice mattered. "We all have our struggles," the mentor said softly. "What's important is that we share them to learn and grow together." The success of this pilot session was a clear indicator that their vision for an international mentorship network was not just idealistic — it was achievable.

Melanie's collaboration with international artists resulted in a digital showcase highlighting the artwork created during their virtual workshops. The online exhibition, titled "Global Echoes," featured diverse art pieces that told stories of loss, resilience, and the hope of a united future. Each piece was accompanied by a short narrative explaining the artist's connection to the theme. The exhibition quickly garnered attention on social media, with viewers worldwide leaving messages of support and sharing their stories. Melanie's excitement was palpable as she monitored the responses, realizing that art had once again served as a bridge connecting hearts across the globe.

The momentum of these initiatives led to a significant turning point: the realization that their movement could serve as a model for global change. In a final virtual meeting, the core team gathered again, joined by several international collaborators. Evan summarized the progress: "We've expanded our local movement into a network that spans continents. Our digital platform is thriving, our international forums are scheduled, and our mentorship pilot shows promising results." His words were met with enthusiastic nods and affirmations from the international partners, whose faces on the screen reflected hope and determination.

Kiera's voice, filled with conviction, added, "Our goal is to create a global community where every voice is heard, regardless of where it comes from. We've learned that isolation is a universal struggle, but so is the need for connection. This forum, these initiatives are not just projects; they're the blueprint for a future where empathy and understanding guide our communities."

The discussion then turned to long-term strategies. They agreed to set up an advisory board with representatives from each participating country, ensuring the movement's growth would be inclusive and culturally sensitive. Plans were laid out for periodic international conferences, where "The Echoes Network" members could gather in person, exchange ideas, and celebrate the power of collective action. They also discussed the possibility of launching a global media campaign to amplify their message, using social media, podcasts, and digital storytelling to reach a broader audience.

The international collaborators expressed their gratitude and excitement as the meeting drew to a close. "This movement," said Lucia, a youth advocate from Spain, "has shown us that when we come together, we can overcome the barriers of language, culture, and distance.

Your vision is our vision — a future where every cry for help is answered, no matter where it originates."

The final moments of the meeting were filled with a shared sense of purpose. Evan, Kiera, Ben, and Melanie knew that while challenges still lay ahead, they had laid the groundwork for something monumental — a network that could bring light to every corner of the world where darkness had once prevailed.

Later that night, as Evan sat alone in his room and reviewed the day's progress, he felt an overwhelming surge of hope. Every new connection, every international conversation, was a testament to the fact that their movement had grown into a global family. "Tyler's memory," he thought, "is not confined to our school — it resonates with everyone who has ever felt alone." With renewed determination, he continued refining the digital platform, ensuring it would be a living, evolving space for shared human experiences.

Kiera, too, found solace in quiet reflection. Sitting at a window in her apartment, she looked over the city. She imagined a future where every community, every school, and every individual had a space to share their story. This space could transform pain into purpose and isolation into unity. "This is our calling," she whispered to herself, "to build bridges that connect hearts across the globe."

Ben and Melanie, each in their way, were equally committed. Ben's mentor network was expanding, and he felt a profound satisfaction in seeing the impact of his efforts ripple outward. Melanie's art was reaching new audiences, and every message of appreciation fueled her creative drive.

Together, the team recognized that they were not merely expanding a local movement but laying the foundation for a global revolution of compassion and connection. The initiatives they were building would, over time, empower individuals everywhere to share their stories and support one another, ensuring that no one ever had to face their struggles alone.

As dawn approached the next day, the group gathered again for a final check-in call. The energy on the screen was contagious — a mix of exhaustion, excitement, and unwavering commitment. Evan concluded the meeting by saying, "We're stepping into a new era where our voices transcend borders, and our shared humanity becomes our greatest strength. Let's carry this momentum forward and ensure that every silent cry worldwide finds its echo."

Kiera's final words were hopeful: "This is the future we're building — a world where every whisper turns into a global chorus of change."

With that, the call ended, leaving each member with a profound sense of purpose. Their journey had taken them from the halls of a small high school to a vision of global connection — a vision that promised to honor Tyler's legacy and transform the lives of countless individuals along the way.

Implementing the Global Blueprint

The momentum of a global vision had transformed from hopeful ideas to actionable plans. As the virtual forums, partnerships, and community outreach initiatives moved forward, Evan, Kiera, Ben, and Melanie immersed themselves in turning their shared blueprint into reality. No longer confined to discussions and planning sessions, they began implementing a network that would carry their message of hope, resilience, and connection across international borders.

It started with pilot virtual forums that brought together young people from diverse cultural backgrounds. Evan had dedicated countless hours to perfecting the technology behind "The Echoes Network," ensuring the platform could support multiple languages and facilitate real-time discussions. On the day of the first forum, the digital room buzzed with anticipation. Participants from countries as varied as Germany, India, Kenya, and Brazil logged in, their faces illuminated by the glow of their screens.

Evan, moderating the session, welcomed everyone warmly. "Today, we bridge continents," he announced, his voice steady and filled with conviction. "We're here to share our stories, struggles, and hopes — because our experiences unite us in our desire to be heard no matter where we come from." As the forum commenced, small groups formed in breakout rooms. In one virtual room, a teenager from Mumbai shared how societal pressures had forced him into silence, while another from Nairobi described the challenge of balancing tradition with modern expectations. Their voices, raw and honest, underscored a universal truth: isolation was not bound by borders.

Meanwhile, Kiera was in constant contact with local partners in her city, finalizing details for the upcoming international forum scheduled for the following summer. Over video calls and emails, she collaborated with representatives from various cultural centers and educational institutions.

One conversation with a representative from a renowned cultural institute in Paris was particularly inspiring. "Our institute has long sought a platform to discuss mental health and identity in a multicultural context," the representative explained. "Your initiative offers a powerful space for that dialogue. We would be honored to host a segment of your forum."

Kiera's eyes lit up. With every new partner secured, the vision of a rotating international forum became more tangible — a platform where diverse communities could come together, share their unique challenges, and learn from one another.

Ben, whose mentorship program had already garnered local success, now faced the challenge of scaling it globally. He had been working on a pilot project that paired mentors from his region with students in a remote part of Eastern Europe. The logistics were complicated — time zone differences, language barriers, and varying educational contexts posed significant hurdles. However, during one test session, something remarkable happened. A young student who had previously been too timid to share his struggles finally opened up about the difficulties of adjusting to a new educational system. His mentor, an empathetic high school graduate with a personal history of overcoming isolation, listened intently and shared his own story of adaptation. "I know what it feels like to be lost in a new world," the mentor said softly. "But together, we can find a way forward."

That session marked a turning point: even with the challenges of distance and difference, the power of one-on-one connection shone through. Ben began to document every success story, determined to refine and expand the program to serve as a model for other regions.

At the same time, Melanie was spearheading an ambitious collaboration with international artists. After weeks of virtual workshops and creative exchanges, she had orchestrated a joint project called "Global Echoes." This initiative invited artists worldwide to contribute pieces that spoke to themes of isolation, hope, and the resilience of the human spirit. In coordinated sessions, artists shared their techniques, cultural narratives, and personal journeys. One muralist from South Africa demonstrated how local history and traditional art could blend to create a vivid, contemporary expression of communal pain and hope. Another poet from Japan recited verses that bridged ancient traditions with modern struggles. The collaborative effort resulted in a digital gallery that was both stunning and profoundly moving — a visual narrative that showcased the diversity of human experience and the unifying power of art.

Melanie's digital gallery was not meant to stand alone as the project evolved. She planned to create a traveling exhibition to tour international cities, allowing communities to experience the art in person and discuss the universal challenges of mental health and isolation. The idea was met with enthusiastic support from cultural institutions in several countries, and soon, Melanie was coordinating with curators, sponsors, and local artists to finalize the logistics.

At the heart of the movement, the team reconvened regularly to align their efforts and share progress. Evan summarized the day's successes and challenges in one late-night video call. "We're breaking down barriers," he said, his voice filled with determination. "Every forum we host, every new partner we secure, every mentorship session that makes a difference reinforces our belief that these stories matter. But we must keep our focus: we aim to ensure that no one, anywhere, feels unheard."

Kiera, always the steady voice of reason, added, "We have the vision and the passion, but we must also be adaptable. Different cultures have different needs. Our next step is to gather feedback from our international partners, adjust our strategies, and ensure that every component of our movement is culturally sensitive and effective." The call for adaptability resonated with the team; they knew that their initiatives had to respect and incorporate local nuances to create a global impact.

In the following days, the team's international outreach efforts began to bear fruit. Evan's digital platform saw a surge of activity from users in diverse countries. New submissions, in languages ranging from Spanish to Mandarin, began appearing — each one a unique perspective on the shared human experience of isolation and hope. Kiera's efforts resulted in signing several memoranda of understanding with international youth organizations. Ben's pilot mentorship program reported promising outcomes, with several successful pairings underway. Melanie's art collaboration was featured in a popular global online magazine, drawing accolades from across the globe.

The team held a pivotal virtual conference with all their international partners as the global projects advanced. The conference was a mosaic of voices from around the world — a mixture of recorded testimonials, live presentations, and interactive Q&A sessions. At one point, a representative from India shared, "In our community, many young people struggle with the stigma of mental health. Your movement offers a way to break that cycle, to show that speaking up is not a weakness but a strength." The shared sentiments reinforced the team's conviction: the movement was not just local but a universal call for empathy and action.

The virtual conference concluded with a collective commitment to collaborate on an annual global summit that would bring together youth leaders, mental health experts, artists, and community organizers from every participating country. This tentatively titled "Voices United" summit was envisioned as a forum for exchanging ideas, celebrating successes, and forging new partnerships. The announcement of the summit sent ripples of excitement through the digital platform and across social media, cementing the movement's status as a rising global force.

Late one evening, after the conference had ended and the screens had gone dark, Evan sat quietly in his room, reflecting on their achievements. He thought of Tyler — a quiet boy whose silence had sparked a revolution — and felt an overwhelming sense of gratitude and responsibility. "We've come so far," he whispered, "and yet, there's so much more to do." His fingers danced over the keyboard as he drafted a message for the next phase of the digital campaign that would invite even more people to join their global dialogue.

Across the ocean, Kiera, too, was in quiet contemplation. Sitting by her window with a steaming cup of tea, she reviewed the feedback from the international forums and the community meetings. The diversity of voices and the shared experiences were a testament to the universality of their mission. "Our movement is not just a spark — it's a beacon," she murmured. "A beacon that will light the way for countless others to step out of silence and into a future of connection and hope."

Having just concluded another successful mentorship session, Ben felt the warmth of transformation. His work had expanded beyond a local initiative, now part of a more extensive, interconnected support network. With each favorable outcome, every student who found the courage to share their story reaffirmed their belief that change was possible when individuals came together. "We're proving that isolation is not permanent," he thought. "Our voices, when united, can create a legacy of care."

And Melanie, ever the creative spirit, found inspiration in every new collaboration. As she prepared for another virtual workshop with artists from different continents, she realized that art was the thread that wove their global movement together. "Our collective creativity can heal," she said during one online session. "It's a language that transcends all barriers, uniting us in our shared humanity." Her contagious passion inspired even the most hesitant participants to open up and contribute their unique perspectives.

In the following weeks, the efforts to build global connections consolidated into a coherent, actionable framework. The Echoes Network was upgraded with multilingual support, the virtual forums became regular events, and the mentorship program's pilot phase reported promising results. Each initiative, while distinct, was interlinked — forming a robust network that connected diverse communities through the common goal of ensuring that every voice was heard.

As the day of the global summit approached, the team gathered one final time for a virtual strategy session. The atmosphere was intense and hopeful — a mix of nerves and determination. Evan summarized the progress: "We've established connections in every corner of the world. Our digital platform is thriving, our mentorship program is expanding, and our international forums have already begun to change lives. Now, we prepare to unite everyone at the global summit — a true celebration of united voices."

Kiera added, "Our movement was born from a need to break the silence at River Valley High. Today, we extend that mission to the world. Every voice and story is a piece of a larger mosaic that tells the tale of human resilience and connection."

Their voices, steady and resolute, echoed through the digital conference room, forging a collective commitment to the journey ahead. The plan for the global summit was set in motion, with invitations sent to youth leaders, mental health experts, and community organizers from around the world. It was a bold step that the team embraced whole heartedly — knowing that the challenges of scaling a movement were far outweighed by the potential to transform lives globally.

That evening, as the virtual meeting ended and the screens went dark, Evan stared at the last line of his draft message, "Our voices are the legacy of our shared humanity," and felt a profound sense of purpose. Kiera reflected on the journey from the quiet halls of River Valley to this expansive global vision, her heart swelling with hope. Ben thought of every student who had ever felt isolated, and Melanie imagined a world where art and creativity bridged every divide.

As dawn broke the next day, the promise of a global movement shone brightly. The digital platform, the mentorship network, and the international forums were all poised to create ripples extending far beyond their immediate communities. The vision of "Voices United" was no longer a distant dream — it was an emerging reality built on the unwavering belief that every silent cry could ignite a revolution of hope.

Stepping into this new day, the team felt the weight of their responsibilities and the boundless possibilities before them. The global connections they had forged were not merely partnerships; they were a network of hope, a tapestry of stories that would redefine how communities engaged with mental health and resilience. With every new contact and every shared insight, the movement grew stronger, affirming that the legacy of their past struggles could light the path to a future where every voice from every corner of the globe would be celebrated.

In that final moment, as Evan, Kiera, Ben, and Melanie prepared to embark on the next phase of their journey, they knew that the work ahead was immense. Yet, buoyed by the support of a global community and driven by the memory of a quiet boy whose silence had sparked it all, they stepped forward with unyielding determination. "We're not just changing our community," Evan declared, "we're paving the way for a world where no one ever has to suffer in silence."

Kiera smiled a blend of gratitude and fierce resolve in her eyes. "This is our promise: that every story, every whisper, every cry for help, will be transformed into a global anthem of hope."

With that, the team closed their final virtual session of the day, each member inspired by the realization that their voices — now connected across continents — were part of a global legacy destined to echo far into the future.

Transforming Global Connections: Empowering Local Voices

As the momentum of international outreach solidified into a robust network, the next challenge emerged: transforming global connections into tangible local empowerment. With "The Echoes Network" now serving as a digital bridge linking voices from around the world, Evan, Kiera, Ben, and Melanie knew that the accurate measure of their success would be how effectively they could adapt these global ideas to serve the unique needs of individual communities.

In a bustling community center in a vibrant urban neighborhood, Kiera convened a meeting with local organizers, educators, and youth leaders who had long struggled with issues of isolation and underrepresentation. The room was a mosaic of diverse faces and perspectives — each individual's story of resilience and a deep-seated desire for change. Kiera began by addressing the group, her voice calm yet resolute.

"Our movement started with a personal tragedy, a silent cry from a friend we lost," she said, her eyes sweeping the room. "Today, we stand not only as witnesses but as active participants in transforming that loss into a source of strength. The global connections we've forged remind us that isolation is universal — but so is the need for support. We want to empower our local community with the tools, knowledge, and empathy we've gathered on our journey."

The meeting room buzzed with conversation as participants discussed integrating the global best practices from "The Echoes Network" into locally relevant programs. One organizer from the neighborhood, Maria, shared her perspective: "In our community, many young people feel that their voices are not valued. By adopting strategies that have worked internationally, we can tailor them to our cultural context. We need training sessions, resource centers, and support groups to make everyone feel seen and heard."

By joining via a live video link from his laptop, Evan contributed his ideas with quiet conviction. "Our digital platform has been a powerful tool," he explained. "But its success depends on its accessibility and relevance to local needs. I propose we develop a series of local ambassadors — community members who can help translate the global dialogue into actionable, locally tailored programs. These ambassadors will receive active listening, conflict resolution, and digital literacy training to help their peers navigate the online space and connect it with real-world support."

Kiera nodded thoughtfully. "That's an excellent idea," she said. "Local ambassadors can bridge the global movement and the day-to-day challenges our community faces. We need to ensure that every initiative is not just imposed from above but co-created with those most affected."

Busy at a local school, Ben visited classrooms and spoke directly with students about the mentorship network. In a bright, airy classroom, he met with a group of middle schoolers, listening intently as they shared their struggles. One student, Asha, hesitated before speaking: "Sometimes, I feel like my voice doesn't matter because I come from a family where English isn't our first language. I'm scared to speak up because I worry people won't understand."

Ben leaned forward, his tone gentle yet determined. "Asha, you are important. Your voice has power, and I want you to know that many of us have faced similar challenges. Our mentorship program is designed so no one has to face their struggles alone. We're here to listen, support, and help you find your strength." His words resonated in the silent room as the students exchanged glances and tentative smiles. The connection was immediate — a small victory in transforming isolation into empowerment.

Meanwhile, Melanie was spearheading a collaborative project with a local art collective. She led a workshop in a converted warehouse turned creative space that brought together regional artists and community members to create public art installations. The workshop was alive with energy: canvases, spray paints, and various colors transformed the blank walls into vibrant expressions of hope and resilience.

During a break, one of the artists, Ravi, explained his vision: "Art can give voice to the voiceless. When you see your story on a wall, it becomes real — a part of the community's identity."

Melanie nodded in agreement, adding, "Our global art collaborations have shown us that creativity can bridge cultural divides. Now, we're taking that same energy and tailoring it to reflect the unique spirit of your neighborhood."

As the day unfolded, the local initiatives began to take shape. Kiera organized an "Empowerment Circles" series in community centers, where residents gathered to share their experiences and co-create solutions. These circles were designed to be inclusive and adaptable, incorporating techniques learned from international forums but modified to fit local customs and needs.

One Empowerment Circle, held in a small community hall adorned with hand-painted murals, featured discussions on mental health, identity, and the power of storytelling. The session was moderated by a local teacher who had undergone training as part of the digital platform's ambassador program. As participants shared their narratives, the room was filled with unity and collective healing — a microcosm of what the global movement aspired to achieve.

Back at his desk later that afternoon, Evan worked on integrating new features into "The Echoes Network." He was determined to make the platform as inclusive and user-friendly as possible. Collaborating with a small team of volunteer developers, he added options for regional language support and local resource directories. Every update was tested and refined, ensuring that the digital experience was a mirror of global stories and a practical tool for local empowerment. "Our goal is to create a seamless connection between online dialogue and offline action," he explained to his team. "We want our users to feel that they're not just reading about change — they're part of it."

In a subsequent virtual meeting, Kiera and Evan convened with representatives from various local organizations to assess the progress of the integrated initiatives. The conversation was productive, focusing on both successes and challenges. One local partner expressed concerns about reaching the most marginalized individuals in the community.

Kiera listened carefully and suggested, "We need to reach out directly — perhaps through door-to-door initiatives or community health drives. Let's partner with local clinics and social workers with a foothold in these areas. Our global connections give us a powerful model, but we must ensure that our solutions are accessible to everyone, especially those who have historically been left out."

The group agreed, and plans were quickly set to launch a pilot outreach program. The program would involve trained ambassadors visiting neighborhoods, hosting small workshops, and distributing resource guides. These guides, which incorporated global best practices and locally relevant information, were designed to empower residents to seek help and share their stories. Evan worked on translating the guides into several regional languages, while Melanie designed visually engaging layouts that made the information easy to digest.

That evening, as the sun set over the community, Kiera took a quiet moment. Sitting on a park bench beneath a sprawling tree, she reflected on the day's accomplishments. The tangible results of their efforts — the empowered individuals, the collaborative art projects, and the newly updated digital platform — filled her with pride and a deep sense of responsibility. "We are not just building programs," she thought. "We are creating a legacy — a network of support that will uplift our community for years to come."

Across town, Ben visited the after-school program at the local community center. He found that many students, inspired by the mentorship initiative, were eager to volunteer as mentors. In a small, brightly lit room, a group of teenagers gathered around Ben as he recounted his journey from silence to action. "Each of you has the power to make a difference," he said. "Your voice matters, and by sharing your story, you can help someone else find their courage." Their eyes shone with a newfound confidence — a clear sign that his words had struck a chord.

In parallel, Melanie continued to refine the plans for the traveling art exhibit. Her vision for a series of public installations was coming together, with local sponsors and artists eager to participate. During one collaborative session at a popular local gallery, she and a group of artists discussed how to capture best the diversity of experiences represented by "The Echoes Network." "We want the art to speak for those who cannot," one artist declared his voice firm. "Let it be a mirror that reflects every shade of human emotion." The sentiment resonated, and detailed plans for the exhibit were drafted — a clear, actionable blueprint that would quickly move from concept to reality.

As the night deepened, the local community's transformation became more evident. The digital platform was live, actively engaging thousands of users, and the feedback was overwhelmingly positive. Residents began to share stories of personal growth and connection — stories that validated the team's efforts and reinforced the belief that every voice truly mattered. Watching the growing number of contributions on the platform, Kiera felt a surge of hope. "This is what we're here for," she murmured. "To ensure that every silent cry is transformed into a message of empowerment."

Later that night, the core team gathered again for a final virtual checkin. The conversation was animated, with each member contributing updates from their projects. Evan reported that the new multilingual features had received praise from users across different regions. At the same time, Kiera shared that the pilot outreach program had already begun to engage previously hard-to-reach communities. Ben announced that the mentorship program had doubled its participation. Melanie revealed that the traveling art exhibit would debut at a local community center in the coming weeks.

"Today," Kiera said, her voice steady and filled with quiet conviction, "we have transformed our global vision into local action. Our efforts are not isolated projects — they are parts of a single, unified movement that will carry the legacy of our past into a brighter, more connected future."

Evan added, "We are proving that global connections can be transformed into real, sustainable change. Every new partnership, every community workshop, every piece of art is a step toward a world where every voice is heard."

The team felt a renewed sense of purpose as they concluded the meeting. There were many challenges ahead, but the foundation they had built was solid. They were not just expanding their movement — they were embedding it into the very fabric of the community, ensuring that the lessons of the past would guide every future endeavor.

Outside, the cool night air carried whispers of possibility as the city settled into a gentle calm. In the quiet moments before sleep, each team member reflected on the day's progress and the promise of a legacy far beyond individual achievements. "We are building bridges," Melanie whispered as she reviewed the day's feedback. "Bridges that will connect every isolated soul with the warmth of a caring community."

And so, with a profound commitment to transforming global ideas into local empowerment, the team stepped into the future. They knew that the journey was just beginning. Still, they also knew that every voice, every connection, and every small act of courage would contribute to a legacy of enduring change. In this legacy, every person could find their place in a world that refused to leave anyone behind.

Empowering the Unheard: Local Implementation and Cultural Integration

In the heart of a vibrant urban neighborhood, where a mosaic of cultures painted the streets, and voices from every corner spoke of history and hope, the international vision of "The Echoes Network" began its careful transformation into locally resonant action. After forging global connections and establishing a digital platform that united voices from around the world, Evan, Kiera, Ben, and Melanie turned their focus toward ensuring that these innovations were not only accessible but also deeply rooted in the specific cultural contexts of the communities they aimed to serve.

It was early one morning when Kiera visited a community center renowned for its rich cultural heritage. The center was a hub for local dialogue, with its colorful murals and freshly brewed coffee mingling with the aroma of home-cooked meals from a nearby diner. Here, community organizers, educators, and long-time residents gathered to discuss local issues and celebrate the diversity that defined them. Kiera had arranged a series of focus groups to understand firsthand the unique challenges these residents faced, particularly in the realm of mental health and social isolation.

A familiar theme emerged as Kiera sat in a circle with community elders and youth. While the global movement spoke of shared pain and collective strength, local voices emphasized the importance of cultural identity. "Our traditions color our stories," one elder explained. "We need solutions that respect our language, customs, and history." Kiera listened intently, scribbling notes in her journal. It was clear that for the international initiatives to succeed, they needed to be carefully adapted — transforming global best practices into programs that resonated with local values and experiences.

Evan worked on technical adaptations for "The Echoes Network." He collaborated with volunteer developers and community translators in his small, makeshift studio filled with computer monitors and multilingual dictionaries. He aimed to create an interface that could switch seamlessly between languages and regional dialects. Evan recalled a message from a user in Brazil who had expressed frustration that their local nuances were lost in translation.

"We cannot have a one-size-fits-all solution," Evan thought. "Our platform must reflect the rich diversity of its users." He spent hours integrating features that allowed for cultural tags, region-specific resource directories, and custom themes that echoed the local art and color palettes. Each new feature was tested with community input, ensuring the digital experience was as warm and welcoming as the neighborhoods it aimed to serve.

Meanwhile, Ben took his mentorship program to the next level by forging direct connections with local schools and youth clubs. In a lively, sunlit classroom at a community center near a bustling market, Ben met with local educators eager to see a program that offered academic support and emotional guidance.

"Our children come from varied backgrounds," one teacher explained, "and often they feel their struggles are unique and insurmountable. A mentorship program that understands your culture and speaks your language can make all the difference."

Ben shared stories of how his previous pairings had improved academic performance and empowered students to embrace their identities. He worked with the teachers to develop a mentorship curriculum incorporating local examples, traditional narratives, and culturally relevant coping strategies. The response was overwhelmingly positive, and soon, a pilot program was launched that paired local mentors with students facing challenges unique to their community. One young mentee, Altha, tearfully admitted later that day, "For the first time, I feel like someone understands where I come from and what I'm going through." That moment, simple and sincere, underscored the transformative power of culturally sensitive mentorship.

In parallel, Melanie collaborated with local artists to expand her vision for community art projects. She organized a historic community center workshop that doubled as an art gallery. The center, adorned with traditional textiles and indigenous crafts, was a living archive of the neighborhood's history. Local muralists, potters, and poets gathered to share their craft, and Melanie facilitated discussions on how art could be used to express both global struggles and local triumphs.

"Art is the language of the soul," one poet declared. "It speaks in colors, symbols, and rhythms that transcend words — but it also carries the weight of our heritage."

Inspired by these conversations, Melanie and the group conceived a series of collaborative murals. Each mural would be designed by artists from the community, with elements that represented local legends, historical events, and everyday resilience. The goal was to beautify public spaces and create a visual narrative that celebrated diversity while uniting the community under a shared banner of hope.

During one particularly inspiring session, an experienced muralist named Radi explained, "When we paint, we tell our collective story. Every brushstroke is a memory — a tribute to those who came before us and a promise to those who will come after."

His words resonated with Melanie; together, they planned a mural to be unveiled at the upcoming local cultural festival. The mural was intended to be interactive: residents could add small symbols or messages, creating an evolved living artwork. This idea captured the imagination of the entire group, symbolizing the fusion of global ideas with local tradition.

Later that afternoon, the core team reconvened for a joint strategy session with representatives from various local organizations. The group discussed ways to further adapt the global blueprint to their local reality in a spacious room lined with books and photographs of the community's history.

Kiera emphasized the importance of genuinely listening to the community's needs. "We have a wealth of ideas from our international partners, but we must also honor the voices of those who live here daily," she stated. "Let's create a feedback loop where every initiative is continuously refined based on local input."

Evan agreed, noting that technology could facilitate this process through surveys, community polls, and interactive workshops hosted on "The Echoes Network." Together, they outlined a plan to launch a series of community engagement events — from local art exhibitions and public forums to small-scale mentorship gatherings — that would serve as pilot projects for broader implementation.

One of the most compelling outcomes of this session was the decision to form a local advisory board. Composed of community elders, educators, local artists, and youth representatives, the board would bridge global ideas and local action. Its role was to ensure that every initiative, whether digital or on the ground, was culturally appropriate and met the community's real needs. The board would meet regularly to review progress, suggest adaptations, and help secure additional funding through local grants and sponsorships.

As the evening approached, the team's work crystallized into tangible projects. Evan's updated digital platform, now enriched with regional languages and culturally relevant resources, was set for a public beta launch. Ben's mentorship pilot had already received enthusiastic feedback from mentors and mentees, and plans were underway to expand the program to neighboring districts. Melanie's collaborative art project was scheduled to debut at the community festival next month, and Kiera's series of empowerment workshops was set to launch in local community centers.

That night, as Kiera walked along a tree-lined street, she paused to reflect on the day's achievements. The cool night air was filled with the soft hum of the city — a reminder that change, though challenging, was a constant, living force. "Every local voice matters," she whispered, thinking of the community members whose stories had enriched their plans. "Our global vision is only as strong as its roots in our neighborhood." In that moment, she felt a profound sense of responsibility — not only to carry the legacy of their movement but to ensure that it resonated with the people who had lived the struggles they sought to overcome.

Evan reviewed feedback from early users of the updated platform. The responses were overwhelmingly positive: users praised the ease of navigating the site in their language, the relevance of local resource links, and the warmth of the design. "This is the start of something real," he murmured to himself, feeling both relief and excitement at the prospect of their vision taking shape in the real world.

Over the next few days, the local advisory board convened for its inaugural meeting. In a room filled with earnest discussions and hopeful faces, the board members shared insights from their own experiences. One elder, a respected community historian, stressed the importance of preserving local traditions while embracing new ideas. "We must remember," he said, "that our community's strength lies in our heritage. By combining that heritage with the innovative approaches of your global network, you create something truly transformative."

The board's input led to several key adaptations. The mentorship program would incorporate traditional storytelling sessions, allowing mentors and mentees to share their struggles and the cultural narratives that had sustained their communities for generations. The art projects would feature elements celebrating local history — symbols, motifs, and colors resonating with the neighborhood's identity. The empowerment workshops would include sessions on both modern mental health techniques and traditional practices, such as community rituals that fostered unity and healing.

The team felt a deep sense of purpose as these plans were set into motion. Their vision was no longer an abstract, global ideal — it had become a living, breathing part of their local reality. Every initiative, every partnership, and every adaptation proved to be a testament to the power of integrating global inspiration with local authenticity. They were building bridges that spanned geographical distances and connected hearts and minds across cultural divides.

That night, as the community center's lights dimmed and the city settled into a gentle calm, Evan, Kiera, Ben, and Melanie gathered again — this time to review the progress of their local adaptations. They sat around a long table, poring over detailed reports, community feedback forms, and proposals for upcoming events. The air was filled with quiet excitement; no matter how small, every success story was a victory in their ongoing mission to empower the unheard.

Evan closed his laptop with a satisfied smile. "We're making a difference," he said, his voice steady with hope. "Our global vision is taking root here, and every step we take is building a foundation for lasting change." Kiera nodded in agreement, adding, "This isn't just about technology or programs — it's about people. It ensures everyone in the community feels seen, valued, and empowered."

Ben and Melanie shared their updates — stories of breakthroughs in mentorship and art that echoed with the promise of a brighter future. Together, the team celebrated their progress, aware that the journey was far from over but buoyed by the collective strength of their community.

As they parted ways that evening, each team member carried with them the conviction that their movement would continue to grow — nurtured by the deep connections they had forged and the enduring spirit of the community. "Our legacy is built on the power of local voices," Kiera whispered as she walked home under the starlit sky.

"And by honoring our roots, we can inspire change far beyond these streets."

In the quiet that followed, the promise of a new, inclusive future shone brightly — a future where global connections and local empowerment worked hand in hand to create a world in which every silent cry would be met with the warmth of collective support, every isolated voice would find a place in the chorus of community. Every individual would know that they truly mattered.

A World United – The Global Legacy

The early morning sky was streaked with soft hues of orange and lavender, signaling a new day for communities that had once lived in silence. In the wake of a transformative journey that began within the walls of River Valley High, the movement had now grown into a global force — a legacy built on the raw power of human connection and empathy. This was when Evan, Kiera, Ben, and Melanie's dreams of a local revolution blossomed into a global legacy.

In a modest studio in a busy urban center, Evan reviewed the latest data streaming from "The Echoes Network." The digital platform had become a living archive of human experience — stories in dozens of languages submitted by people from every corner of the globe. Each entry was a testament to the shared struggles and triumphs of those who had felt isolated, judged, or ignored. As he scrolled through testimonials, Evan recalled the words that had once haunted him: "I feel invisible," "No one sees me," and "I'm drowning in silence." Today, however, those words have taken on a new meaning. They were no longer a lament; they had become the rallying cries of a global community united in hope.

With a deep breath, Evan prepared a new announcement for the platform — a call to action for the global community. "We are more than a collection of stories," he typed carefully, "We are a movement. Every voice here matters, and together, we can build a future where every cry for help is met with compassion." He paused, his fingers hovering above the keyboard, feeling the weight of his responsibility. When he finally pressed "post," the message rippled across the network, igniting conversations in online forums, social media, and beyond.

Half a world away, in a bustling European city, Kiera sat in a sunlit café, her eyes scanning a handwritten letter from a local youth worker. The letter described how a small group of teenagers in her neighborhood had come together to create their version of "Voice Circles" — safe spaces to share their dreams and fears. The youth worker wrote, "Your movement has shown us that there is strength in speaking out even in our darkest moments. We no longer feel alone." Kiera smiled, feeling that familiar blend of bittersweet remembrance and hope. She had always believed that change was possible when people dared to share their truth, and now, seeing that belief take root in another corner of the world, she felt reinvigorated.

That afternoon, Ben hosted a virtual call with mentors and mentees from several countries. The call was a vibrant mosaic of faces, each carrying a unique story of struggle and resilience. One young girl from India, her eyes bright despite the challenges described, shared how the mentorship program had helped her overcome the stigma of mental health in her community. "I used to feel like my voice was a burden," she admitted softly. "But now, I see that every word I speak can be a beacon for someone else." The call was filled with nods and quiet affirmations, a reminder that their initiative was no longer confined to local boundaries — it was a bridge connecting hearts and minds worldwide. Ben listened intently, realizing that every connection he forged was a small victory in the war against isolation.

Meanwhile, Melanie had been tirelessly working with international artists to finalize plans for a traveling exhibition showcasing art inspired by the movement. In her studio, filled with canvases and sketches from diverse cultures, she pieced together a thematic collage titled "Global Echoes." The exhibition would feature murals, digital installations, and performance art pieces created by artists from Africa, Asia, Europe, and the Americas — each work is a unique reflection of local experiences interwoven with the universal call for empathy and justice. Melanie's vision was clear: art, in all its forms, could transcend language and cultural barriers, uniting disparate communities under the banner of hope.

As evening fell, the team gathered for a final virtual conference with their international partners — a mosaic of voices from every continent. The conference call was a powerful scene: live testimonials, cultural performances, and panel discussions that addressed the universal struggle against isolation and the transformative power of community.

Lucia, a youth advocate from Spain, passionately declared,

"Your movement is a mirror reflecting our collective pain and resilience. We build bridges that span even the deepest divides when we share our stories." Her words resonated deeply, echoing the unity that defined their mission.

The conference moved seamlessly from heartfelt dialogue to practical planning. Ideas flowed freely: plans for regional workshops, cultural exchange programs, and a rotating global summit titled "Voices United." The summit, as envisioned, would bring together youth leaders, mental health experts, and creative minds from across the globe to celebrate shared humanity. Evan and Kiera presented a detailed proposal outlining the logistics, funding models, and collaborative frameworks required to make the summit a reality. The discussion was intense yet hopeful — each participant understood that the challenges ahead were immense, but so was the potential for transformative change.

In one breakout session, a young leader from Kenya spoke about integrating traditional healing practices with modern mental health strategies. "Our ancestors passed down wisdom in stories and rituals," he said, his voice carrying both reverence and determination. "By combining that with the innovative approaches you've developed, we can create a model that respects our heritage while embracing the future." His words underscored a critical point: the global movement must honor local traditions to be genuinely inclusive.

The team's preparations reached a fever pitch as the virtual summit approached. Invitations were sent, schedules finalized, and the global summit, "Voices United," was set to be a landmark event that would bring together hundreds of youth leaders, mental health advocates, and cultural ambassadors. The summit was more than an event — it manifested years of hard work, heartbreak, and the relentless drive to ensure every silent cry was heard.

In the final hours before the summit, Evan hosted a rehearsal session on "The Echoes Network" to test all the new features. Participants from various countries logged in, their faces lighting up as they navigated the platform in their native languages. The live chat buzzed with messages of excitement and anticipation, and Evan felt a deep sense of fulfillment, knowing their vision was now a vibrant reality.

Kiera joined the session, her presence a stabilizing force. "This is it," she said, her voice soft but firm. "Our global vision is coming alive. Every story shared, every connection made, is a testament to our collective strength." Her words were met with virtual applause, and for a moment, the digital space transformed into a global gathering — a community bound not by geography but by the shared commitment to change.

As the summit finally commenced, the energy was electric. The online platform hosted keynote speeches, breakout sessions, and cultural performances that resonated with the universal language of hope. Every contribution, whether a heartfelt testimonial or a powerful piece of art, reinforced the idea that the movement was a living, breathing entity that would continue to grow and evolve with every new voice added to its chorus.

Later that evening, as the virtual summit wound down and the last speakers concluded their addresses, the team gathered for a final reflection. Evan, Kiera, Ben, and Melanie sat together in a quiet virtual room, their faces illuminated by the soft glow of their screens. "Today," Evan began, "we witnessed the power of a truly global movement — a movement where every cry, every story, transcends borders and creates a symphony of hope."

Kiera added, "Our work is far from over, but this summit has shown us that change is possible when we come together. We're not just sharing our stories; we're building a future where every voice is valued, and every individual can find strength in connection."

Ben smiled, his expression serene. "Every step we take from here will build on today's success. Our legacy is not confined to a single school or community — it's a promise that resonates worldwide."

Melanie concluded, "Let our art, our voices, and our shared hope be the guiding light for a future where silence is replaced by unity, and every whisper becomes a global anthem for change."

As the virtual summit ended and the digital room gradually emptied, the impact of the day's events lingered like a warm glow — a testament to the transformative power of global connection. The team knew the journey ahead would be filled with challenges, but they were emboldened by the collective promise of a future where every voice was heard.

They logged off with a final, unspoken agreement, each carrying the profound realization that their global legacy was only beginning. The movement they had sparked, born out of personal loss and nurtured by a deep commitment to empathy, was poised to change lives on a scale they had once only dreamed of. And in that quiet, hopeful moment, the world felt just a little more connected — a little less alone.

Chapter 9: Personal Journeys & Internal Transformations

Echoes of the Past

The morning light filtered softly through the curtains of Evan's small apartment, casting long, gentle shadows across his cluttered desk. Today, as with many other mornings, Evan sat in quiet contemplation, surrounded by remnants of the movement that had reshaped his life. His digital archive — "The Echoes Network" — continued to pulse with new stories and reflections, each post a testament to voices that had once been silenced. Yet amidst this vibrant tapestry, Evan's mind kept returning to one echo defining the beginning of their journey: Tyler's quiet plea, the whisper that had sparked a revolution.

Evan's thoughts drifted back to that fateful day when he first heard Tyler murmur, "I feel like I don't belong," in the aftermath of gym class — a moment that later shattered his complacency and filled him with a deep-seated regret. It was a confession so small yet so potent it became the seed for everything that followed. As he scrolled through the archive, he found himself pausing at each entry, each personal story from students who shared similar feelings of isolation and despair. In those moments, Evan recognized that Tyler's silence was not an isolated tragedy but a symptom of a far more pervasive problem — a world in which too many voices were left unheard.

In a flashback that played like a faded film, Evan remembered sitting in the nearly empty library at River Valley High. The corridors were filled with muted conversations and the soft rustle of pages. He recalled the heavy silence that had enveloped the school after Tyler's loss. This silence was punctuated only by the desperate, unanswered questions of those who had known him, however briefly. That silence had driven him to create "The Echoes Network," a digital space where every whisper of regret and every cry for help was recorded as a testament to the need for change. Years later, that same project had grown into a living, breathing monument to the power of vulnerability.

Evan's gaze shifted to the framed photograph on his desk — a candid shot of Tyler, taken during a moment of rare, unguarded laughter. The image was a bittersweet reminder of what had been lost. "Tyler, if only we'd listened," he murmured under his breath, the memory of that quiet plea resonating in his heart. With a calm intensity, he resolved to honor Tyler's legacy by ensuring that every silent cry would be met with a voice that cared — a promise he carried into every new project and initiative.

Meanwhile, Kiera found herself wrestling with her reflections in the solitude of her room. The vibrant energy of the movement had brought her accolades and recognition as a leader, but with that came a heavy burden of personal regret. In her journal, Kiera poured out the moments she wished she could reclaim — the times when caught up in the whirlwind of responsibilities, she had failed to see the subtle signs of pain in her friends. One entry in particular, written in the quiet hours of a sleepless night, read: "I was too busy leading, too caught up in the noise of expectations, to notice the silent suffering of the one person who needed us most." Those words haunted her, fueling her commitment to never let such oversight occur again.

Kiera remembered the many afternoons she had spent in the empty classrooms of River Valley High, where her leadership had often meant sacrificing her emotional well-being. The memory of Tyler — so gentle, so profoundly alone — had been a constant companion during those times. And as she reread her journal, Kiera realized that personal healing was not a linear path. It was a mosaic of regrets, lessons, and small victories. Every missed moment and every silent apology contributed to a broader understanding of what it meant to care for others honestly.

Determined to transform her regrets into a catalyst for growth, Kiera began seeking out new forms of healing. She attended counseling sessions, where she learned that self-forgiveness was essential to any journey toward change. In one session, her counselor told her, "You cannot heal the wounds of others if you don't mend your own." Those words struck a deep chord within her, prompting Kiera to embrace vulnerability as a strength rather than a weakness. Slowly, she began to share her struggles with a close circle of friends — moments of doubt, the weight of responsibility, and the lingering sorrow of a loss that had forever changed her.

In one particularly poignant conversation, Kiera sat with a trusted friend in a quiet corner of a local café. "I still see Tyler's face in every silent moment," she confessed, her eyes glistening with unshed tears. "I wish I could go back and change the things I overlooked. But maybe, just maybe, I can use that regret to fuel a better future." Her friend, reaching across the table, squeezed her hand in quiet solidarity.

"Your strength lies in your willingness to face these truths," the friend said. "It's that courage that will inspire others to speak up, to demand that no one else suffers in silence."

Meanwhile, Ben, who had long borne the weight of his regrets, continued to redefine his identity through acts of service. His mentorship program — once a personal attempt to atone for past biases — had become a lifeline for many young students. Ben recalled the moments when he had felt utterly alone in his guilt — the nights spent questioning whether he could ever truly forgive himself. Over time, however, those moments had transformed into opportunities for healing. In his work with the mentorship program, Ben learned that every act of kindness, every sincere conversation with a student, was a step toward redemption.

"I was lost in silence," he once admitted during a small group meeting. "But now, when I see a young person finding the courage to speak up, I know that my voice — and our shared voices — can heal even the deepest wounds."

Ben's journey was not without its setbacks. There were days when the echoes of his past mistakes reverberated through his mind, making him question whether his efforts were enough. Yet, with each success story — a student overcoming their fear of speaking out, a mentee finding new confidence — Ben's resolve strengthened. He kept a detailed journal of these successes, a living record of how even the smallest act of connection could make a world of difference.

Melanie's creative spirit had evolved into a powerful tool for personal expression and healing. The art that had once been a private refuge for her was now a public declaration of resilience. Melanie spent hours translating her emotions into color and form in her studio, surrounded by canvases and vibrant sketches. Each brushstroke was a tribute to the memories of those who had felt silenced, and every completed piece was a testament to the belief that beauty could emerge from even the darkest moments.

Melanie's artwork was more than just a creative outlet — a dialogue with the past and a bridge to the future. She recalled the days of the Festival of Echoes when public art installations had given voice to the silent struggles of countless students. As she prepared for an upcoming solo exhibition, Melanie saw her work as a continuation of that dialogue. This visual memoir captured the pain of loss and the transformative power of collective hope. She painted a series of overlapping silhouettes in one piece, each representing a person who had once felt unseen. The silhouettes gradually merged into a single, radiant figure — a symbol of unity and the healing power of shared experience.

As these individual journeys unfolded, the common thread that tied them together was the legacy of Tyler — a quiet boy whose unheard cries sparked a movement. His memory was both a source of deep sorrow and a beacon of hope, a reminder that even in the face of loss, every voice had the power to effect change. Tyler's legacy was a constant presence for each of them — a reminder of what they had lost and a call to action for what they could build in its place.

In a series of late-night video calls, the group shared their reflections and discussed how they could support one another's healing. Evan spoke of the importance of the digital archive as a repository of collective pain and promise — a space where every anonymous post was a step toward understanding. Kiera shared her struggles with self-forgiveness and how she was learning to embrace vulnerability as a strength. Ben recounted a recent breakthrough with a mentee who had overcome a deep-seated fear of speaking out. Melanie showed her latest paintings that captured the tumultuous yet hopeful journey they had all shared.

These conversations were raw and unfiltered — an intimate look into the hearts of those who had dedicated themselves to a cause greater than themselves. They were not just planning for the future; they were processing the past, acknowledging their imperfections, and learning that true healing came from within. "We are our work in progress," Kiera remarked in one session, "and every step, every setback, is a part of the process of becoming who we are meant to be."

The day slowly turned into night, and as the group wrapped up their final call for the evening, each member was left with a profound sense of purpose. They realized that their transformations were inextricably linked to the movement they had built — a movement that had started with loss but was now defined by the courage to speak out and the commitment to never let another voice be silenced.

Later that night, as the city lights flickered on and the world outside settled into a quiet slumber, Evan sat alone at his desk. He opened his journal and began to write — a stream of consciousness that captured the day's raw emotions. "Tyler's silence taught us that every unspoken word is a chance missed," he wrote. "But now, every word we share, every cry for help that is heard, builds a legacy of hope. We are rewriting our story, one that will echo through time as a reminder that even the quietest voice has the power to change the world."

Across the city, Kiera, Ben, and Melanie each recorded their reflections, their voices mingling with memories and aspirations. They knew the road ahead would be long and fraught with challenges, but the bonds they had formed — and the lessons they had learned from their internal transformations — would guide them. Their healing journeys were not isolated experiences; they were the foundation upon which their collective future was built.

The promise of a new day filled them with renewed determination as dawn approached. Their legacy, born from the pain of loss and nurtured by the strength of shared stories, was now an integral part of who they were. In that fragile, hopeful moment, they realized that their personal growth was both a tribute to the past and a beacon for the future — a future where every silent cry would be met with the warmth of connection, and every unspoken word would find its echo in the hearts of those who dared to listen.

Overcoming Shadows

The day began with an uneasy stillness that seemed to echo the inner turmoil of those who had carried silent burdens for far too long. In the quiet moments of the early morning, Evan awoke to the soft hum of his alarm — a sound that, on this day, felt like both an ending and a beginning. His room, cluttered with notebooks and remnants of the movement, bore the quiet weight of his thoughts. Today, he resolved, was not just about remembering the pain of the past but about confronting the shadows that had haunted him and transforming that struggle into something resilient.

Evan recalled the long, painful nights when Tyler's quiet cry had first pierced the silence. Those memories were like ghosts — always present, always urging him to do better. Sitting at his desk, he opened his journal and began writing freely, letting the memories spill onto the page without judgment.

Every unspoken word, every silent regret, he wrote, is a weight that can either break us or become the foundation of our strength. In that vulnerable space, he allowed himself to feel the full spectrum of emotions — the sorrow, the anger, the regret — and, most importantly, the budding resolve to channel those emotions into action.

Across town, Kiera found herself in a different kind of solitude. In the dim light of her bedroom, she reviewed old video recordings of her "Voice Circles" at River Valley High, the raw, unedited moments when her peers had bared their hearts in a safe space. Each clip was a reminder of both the vulnerability and the strength that had emerged in those moments. Kiera's eyes filled with tears as she watched a shy student, barely audible, confess that he felt utterly alone despite being surrounded by friends. It was a confession that resonated deeply with her own experiences — the times she had been so overwhelmed by the responsibility that she had failed to see those who needed her truly.

Determined to heal and learn from her past's painful chapters, Kiera began attending counseling sessions. In the soft, confidential space of her therapist's office, she revisited the moments when her ambition had overshadowed her empathy. "I was so busy leading, so consumed with expectations," she admitted during one session, "that I ignored the silent signals of pain. I carry that regret with me but also the determination to change."

Over time, Kiera learned to transform her regret into resolve.

She started a daily practice of reflective journaling and meditation, and slowly, she began to see that embracing her vulnerabilities could be a source of strength rather than a mark of failure.

Ben's journey of self-forgiveness was equally intense. The memories of his missed opportunities — those moments when he had hesitated, remained silent or judged too quickly— were a constant companion. Ben sat with a small group of young mentees one chilly evening at the community center. In the soft glow of a single lamp, a young girl named Laila timidly shared her fear of speaking up, confessing fear of what her peers would think. Ben's heart ached as he imagined how Tyler felt when he had unfairly judged him.

"I understand that fear," he said gently, "because I lived it too. But you cast away some of that darkness every time you express yourself." His simple yet sincere words sparked a subtle shift in the room. Laila's eyes brightened just enough to convey that she believed him, that there was hope in her voice.

Ben later retreated to a quiet corner of the community center and opened an old journal where he had painstakingly recorded his reflections over the past year. He read passages filled with regret and self-reproach, then underlined lines that spoke of the courage he had found in reaching out to others. I didn't understand how words hurt or the impact in failing to listen, he wrote one day. Now, I understand every voice, no matter how small, can change the course of a life. For Ben, each mentoring session, each brave confession from a mentee, was a step away from the shadows of his past — a process of healing that was gradual but inevitable.

Meanwhile, Melanie, whose creativity had long been her refuge, was exploring new ways to express and process her internal struggles. In the quiet solitude of her studio, she let her emotions flow onto large canvases. Unlike her earlier works — vibrant expressions of collective hope and unity — this new series was raw and unfiltered, a visual diary of her internal battles. With each brushstroke, she confronted her fears, regrets, and loss's lingering shadows.

"I paint what I cannot speak," she confided to a close friend during a late-night studio session. "Every color, every shape, is a testament to the strength it takes to overcome the darkness." Her work was deeply personal, yet it resonated with the universal theme of reclaiming one's voice after being silenced by fear and sorrow.

As days turned into weeks, the four friends found that their journeys of overcoming shadows were beginning to intersect in meaningful ways. In regular video calls, they shared updates on their external projects and intimate reflections on their inner battles. Evan talked about how writing had become a cathartic exercise, turning his pain into words that now served as both memorial and motivation. Kiera shared how therapy and meditation had helped her find balance, allowing her to be a leader who listened as much as she guided. Ben recounted small victories in his mentorship program — stories of students who had learned to find their voice despite the echoes of isolation. Melanie also showed her latest paintings, visually exploring the journey from despair to hope.

During one particularly poignant call, the conversation turned to Tyler's legacy. "Tyler's silence was our wake-up call," Evan said, his voice thick with emotion. "But it's also the reminder that every unspoken word can spark change — if we only dare to let it out."

Kiera nodded, adding, "We carry his memory not as a burden but as a call to be better — to see and to listen, even when it's hard."

Their discussions were not without moments of raw vulnerability. In one session, Ben admitted, "There are nights when I feel overwhelmed by the weight of my past mistakes when the shadows seem to whisper that I'll never do enough. But then I see the progress of my mentees, and I remember that healing is a journey that we're all taking together." The room fell silent, each friend reflecting on their struggles and the strength they had found in shared understanding.

Melanie, who had been silent for a long moment, finally spoke. "I used to think my art was just a way to escape the darkness. Now I see it as a bridge — a way to connect with others who have experienced that same darkness and to remind them that there is beauty even in our scars." Her tender and resolute words encapsulated the transformation that had taken root within each of them.

As the call ended, a quiet determination settled over the group. They knew that overcoming the shadows was not a finite battle — it was an ongoing process that required daily acts of courage and compassion. Their journeys, marked by small victories and hard-won insights, were the foundation of the movement they had built together. And in sharing their vulnerabilities, they found that their collective strength was far greater than the sum of their struggles.

Later that night, Evan sat at his desk and reviewed the messages from "The Echoes Network." Each story, each silent cry transformed into a written word, was a reminder of the power of openness. "Our past does not define us," he wrote in his journal, "but by the courage to move forward, to speak up, and to embrace the light that follows even the darkest night." His words resonated with the hope that had been rekindled within him.

Alone in her room, Kiera looked at a framed photograph of Tyler — his eyes gentle and his smile serene, captured in a moment of fleeting happiness. "I promise," she whispered, "that your pleas will not be in vain. Every tear and regret will be transformed into a promise that every voice matters." Her determination was palpable, a quiet vow to lead with empathy and authenticity.

Ben's journal, filled with reflections on mentorship and personal growth, now included pages of sketches and quotes from the students he had mentored. One note read, "Your voice gave me courage to speak." These simple yet profound messages reminded him that every act of vulnerability was a step toward healing. He understood now that the light of connection could soften every shadow of regret.

And Melanie, in her art studio, put the finishing touches on a new series of canvases — a collection that captured the interplay of darkness and light. Each painting was a raw depiction of the struggle to overcome inner demons, yet they also shimmered with hints of hope and renewal. As she stood back to admire her work, she felt deeply grateful for the journey that had brought her here. "Our art," she mused, "is our voice when words fall short. It tells the story of our resilience, our ability to transform pain into beauty."

The journey to overcome the shadows was ongoing; each understood that the healing process was as important as the destination. Their reflections, captured in journals, artworks, and recorded conversations, became a reservoir of strength they could draw on in moments of doubt. We are more than our past, Evan wrote one night, we are the hope we choose to carry forward.

As the chapter on personal transformation progressed, the group recognized that their inner work was a means of healing and a source of inspiration for others. Their stories — painful, honest, and uplifting — began to ripple outward, encouraging those around them to confront their shadows. The message was clear in community workshops, mentoring sessions, and online forums: every silent cry can become a beacon of change when met with courage and connection.

On the final call of the week, as the digital clock ticked toward midnight, the four friends gathered once again in their usual virtual space. The conversation was reflective, filled with the weight of their past and the promise of a future built on resilience. "We've learned that overcoming the shadows isn't about erasing our pain," Kiera said softly, "it's about transforming it into the light that guides us forward."

Evan agreed, adding, "Our voices — when we let them out — can heal not only ourselves but also those who still struggle in silence."

The call ended with each of them feeling a renewed sense of purpose. Their journeys of overcoming shadows had become the bedrock of their collective legacy — a legacy that would continue to inspire, uplift, and empower. As they logged off one by one, the quiet hum of the city outside served as a reminder that, even in darkness, there is always the promise of dawn.

Chapter 10: The Final Voice – Legacy and Closure

The Last Whisper

The sky was a soft canvas of dawn hues as Evan sat on the steps of the old community center — a place that had witnessed the birth and evolution of a movement he once thought was confined to the halls of River Valley High. Years later, every whispered cry from that quiet beginning had grown into a resounding chorus. He held a worn notebook in his hands, its pages filled with memories, regrets, triumphs, and the raw truth of his journey. Today, as he prepared to pen the final chapter of their collective story, he felt both a bittersweet melancholy and a fierce, enduring hope.

Evan's mind drifted back to that fateful day when Tyler's soft, almost imperceptible voice shattered the silence and sparked a movement. He remembered the mix of shock and sorrow, the overwhelming regret he and his friends experienced. That moment, a simple confession of feeling lost, had changed everything. It had forced them to confront the indifference that had long been their world's norm, and it had ignited a fire that, over time, had grown into a global vision. As he reflected on all that had been accomplished, he recognized that Tyler's silence was not just a source of pain but a precious seed of transformation.

Sitting quietly, Evan opened his journal and began to write: *Every silent whisper has led us here — to a moment when we can finally see that our voices, once small and tentative, have become the legacy of a generation. Tyler's quiet plea was the spark, and now, we carry that flame forward in every act of compassion, every word of support, and every shared story of resilience.*

His words were not just reflections on the past but a promise to the future. At that moment, he understood that their movement was not ending; it was evolving. The struggles they had faced the personal battles they had fought, had prepared them to pass on a legacy of hope and empowerment to those who would come after them.

Kiera sat in a sunlit room filled with mementos from her time as a leader at River Valley High. The walls, adorned with photographs of student gatherings, posters from "Voice Circles," and cherished letters of thanks, bore silent testimony to the transformation that had taken place. As she reviewed her journal, Kiera reflected on the many nights she had wrestled with the weight of responsibility — nights when the burden of leadership had almost drowned her in regret for not hearing every silent cry. Now, she saw that each misstep had been a lesson, each moment of vulnerability a steppingstone toward a more compassionate self.

With gentle resolve, Kiera penned in her journal, *I once believed that to lead meant to be infallible, to carry the weight of every heartache alone. But in embracing my imperfections, I discovered the strength of empathy. Every voice I failed to hear has become a part of who I am — guiding me, reminding me that true leadership is sharing our burdens and turning our collective pain into a promise for the future.*

Her words carried a quiet power — a declaration that her healing had become intertwined with the healing of the entire community. For Kiera, the journey was as much about inner transformation as it was about building a legacy. Her renewed sense of self was not defined by past mistakes but by the courage to rise, listen, and love without reservation.

At the local community center where Ben had first found his path to redemption, the echoes of laughter and learning still lingered. Ben, now a mentor whose once-hesitant voice had grown strong and steady, visited the center with a deep purpose. He walked along corridors lined with smiling faces and faded photographs of students who had once felt isolated. In the quiet of an empty classroom, Ben sat down with a group of mentees, their eager eyes reflecting the challenges of their past and the promise of their future. He began to share a story from his journey — a tale of regret that had once paralyzed him with guilt and of his small, courageous steps to overcome it.

"I remember when I didn't realize the power in words," Ben said softly, his voice echoing sincerely. "I didn't understand how badly words can hurt. I didn't listen to what others said. Until it was too late for my friend. But I learned to reach out — each time I offered a kind word or a listening ear — I found that I helped someone. When shared, our voices create a healing network that transcends our pain." The young faces in the room listened intently, each nod and whispered affirmation a silent vow that they, too, would carry forward the legacy of hope.

Ben's words resonated with a quiet strength. In that room, he understood that his journey of self-forgiveness was a beacon for others — a reminder that even the darkest silence could be broken by the light of connection. Every shared story, every small act of vulnerability, was a testament to the transformative power of empathy.

In a bright, art-filled studio on the city's outskirts, Melanie continued to explore the depths of her creative spirit. Her canvases, once a reflection of personal solitude, now burst with a vibrant interplay of colors — a visual narrative of transformation and hope. Standing before a large, evolving mural that captured the journey of their collective healing, Melanie's eyes glistened with quiet pride. The mural was not merely a piece of art but a living story — a tapestry woven from the threads of countless voices, each a reminder that beauty could emerge from even the deepest wounds.

Melanie recorded her thoughts in a small audio journal as she added the final touches. "Every brushstroke tells a story," she said softly into the recorder. "Our art is a testament to the fact that even in our quietest moments, there is a strength that can carry us forward. I paint not to erase the pain, but to honor it — transforming every shadow into a spark of light that guides us toward a future where every voice is cherished."

That morning, as the four friends gathered for one of their final video calls — a ritual that had become a lifeline in their journey — there was a palpable sense of hope mixed with reflective quiet. The screen displayed their tired but resolute faces, each marked by the experiences of their transformations. Evan shared that every word he wrote had become a bridge connecting his past to his future, while Kiera spoke of the healing power found in self-forgiveness. Ben recounted breakthrough moments with his mentees, and Melanie shared her latest artistic triumphs.

"We have all faced our shadows," Evan said, his voice both soft and resolute, "and in doing so, we have found the strength to move forward. Our journey has not been easy, but every step has brought us closer to a truth we must hold: that every silent cry, every hidden sorrow, can be transformed into a beacon of hope when met with courage."

Kiera added, "This is the dawn of a new self — not defined by past regrets but by the power to create, love, and lead with compassion. Our experiences, both painful and profound, have become the foundation of who we are. And it is this strength that we carry into every tomorrow."

Ben's gentle reassurance, "I used to fear that my words would haunt me forever, but now I see that every time I speak up, I become a part of something greater," was met with nods of agreement.

Melanie's final words, "Our art, our voices, our shared vulnerability — they are the legacy of our journey, a promise that we will never let silence define us again," resonated deeply with each of them.

As the call ended, the final echoes of their conversation lingered in the digital space — a collective promise that the journey of healing was ongoing, that every step forward was a victory over the shadows of the past. At that moment, as the light of dawn filtered through their respective windows, Evan, Kiera, Ben, and Melanie embraced a profound truth: that the transformation of self was not an endpoint but the beginning of a legacy. This legacy would inspire others to break their silences and to step boldly into a future where every voice mattered.

The morning that followed was quiet yet full of promise. Each friend carried the tender strength of their renewed selves, ready to face the challenges of a new day. The memories of the past, once a source of deep sorrow, had become the stepping stones of their resilience. And as they each set out into the world, they did so with hearts emboldened by the conviction that personal renewal was the most potent force for lasting change.

In that enduring promise lay the final truth of their journey: that even the quietest whisper, nurtured by self-acceptance and the courage to share its truth, can echo across time and space —

transforming pain into a legacy of hope and silence into a powerful call for connection.

A Legacy That Endures: The Final Chorus

The horizon blushed with the tender hues of early morning as the final echoes of the night faded into gentle dawn. In the grand hall of the civic center — now transformed into a sanctuary of remembrance and celebration — the community gathered one last time to witness the culmination of a journey that had begun with a single, quiet cry and blossomed into a legacy of empowerment. Every banner, every mural, every soft-spoken testimonial was a testament to the enduring impact of a movement born from tragedy and nurtured by unwavering hope.

Evan stood on the stage, his gaze sweeping over the assembled crowd. The faces before him, lit by the warm glow of dawn and the remnants of the previous night's celebration, were the living proof of change. "Today," he began, his voice steady and imbued with quiet strength, "we do not just remember a time of loss — we celebrate a legacy that has transformed our lives and community. Tyler's silence, which once echoed in the empty halls of River Valley High, has become the spark that ignited a chorus of voices. With your unique stories and heartfelt courage, each of you has helped create a world where every cry for help is met with compassion."

The crowd listened in rapt silence as Evan continued. He spoke of the journey — of the long nights spent capturing anonymous confessions on "The Echoes Network," of the countless "Voice

Circles" that turned solitary grief into shared strength, and of the personal battles that each member had fought and overcome. His words resonated with those who had once felt invisible, now united in their determination to ensure that no one would ever be left unheard again.

Across the stage, Kiera took a deep breath and stepped forward. "Our journey was not easy," she admitted, her eyes reflecting sorrow and fierce determination. "There were moments when the weight of responsibility and regret seemed unbearable — when every missed opportunity to listen felt like a failure. But through it all, we learned that true leadership is not about perfection but the willingness to embrace our imperfections and use them as the foundation for change." Her voice wavered slightly as she recalled the many nights of introspection, the long hours spent in silent remorse that gradually transformed into a commitment to empathy. "We have come to understand that every voice matters, and every silent cry calls us to improve. Today, we honor our past and forge a future where everyone is valued."

Ben, whose journey from guilt to redemption had inspired many, then shared his reflections with quiet conviction. "For years, I carried the weight of my words — moments when I hesitated, when fear held me back from reaching out," he began, his voice soft yet clear. "But I've learned that in every act of connection, I was building a bridge from my darkness to someone else's light every time I chose to speak up or simply listen. I stand here today, not as a man defined by his regrets, but as a mentor who has seen the transformative power of a single, kind word. Every story we've shared and every cry we've turned into a conversation proves that our vulnerabilities are our greatest strengths. They have united and given us the power to heal ourselves and our entire community."

Then, with a gentle smile, Melanie stepped into the light. "Art has always been my refuge — a way to give form to my emotions when words were not enough," she said, her eyes glistening with memories of canvases filled with pain and beauty. "But over time, I realized that art is also a way to connect — to translate personal sorrow into a universal language that speaks to every heart. Our collaborative murals, the "Festival of Echoes", and every piece we've created together are not just expressions of our struggles; they are symbols of our resilience. They remind us that even in our darkest moments, a spark of creativity can light the way to a brighter future." Her voice grew firmer, resonating with passion, "Let our art be the enduring reminder that every brushstroke of hope can transform the silence into a symphony of voices that refuse to be ignored."

As the speeches drew close, the stage fell silent for a moment — a silence heavy with reflection and anticipation. Then, as if on cue, the digital screens scattered throughout the hall lit up with a montage of testimonials from "The Echoes Network." The images, a kaleidoscope of faces and emotions from every community corner, played against soft, stirring music. Each testimonial, each captured moment of vulnerability, was a thread in the fabric of their collective legacy.

In that poignant moment, the audience rose to their feet. Applause filled the hall — a powerful, unifying sound that echoed like a final chorus of hope. The applause was not just for the speeches or the grand event; it was a tribute to every life touched by the movement, to every soul that had found the courage to break free from silence.

Outside the hall, as the event concluded and the crowd began to disperse into the cool embrace of the early morning, the impact of the night lingered in the air like a promise. Groups of people huddled in small clusters, discussing the event, sharing their stories, and reaffirming the bonds they had forged through their shared struggles. Tears glistening in his eyes, a local community leader whispered to a friend, "Tonight, I saw a future where every child, every person, will know that their voice matters — that they are never alone."

Later that night, Evan found himself on the steps of the civic center, the soft murmur of the departing crowd still echoing behind him. He gazed up at the starry sky, feeling the profound weight of the legacy they had built. "This," he thought, "is more than just an event. It's the culmination of every silent cry, every moment of despair turned into a declaration of hope. It is our final chorus — a promise that Tyler's legacy will live on in every heart that dares to speak up." With that thought, he closed his journal and smiled, a quiet, determined smile that held the promise of many tomorrows.

As the first light of a new day filtered through the horizon, the community gathered the previous night carried the powerful affirmation of a legacy that would endure. The digital archive, the art installations, and the public forums were now more than just initiatives; they embodied a movement that had transformed personal pain into a global legacy of empowerment and connection.

In that transformative dawn, Evan, Kiera, Ben, and Melanie knew their journey was far from over. Their paths, once defined by silence and regret, had merged into a shared vision — a vision of a future where every voice, no matter how quiet, would be celebrated, and every cry for help would be met with a chorus of support. Their legacy was not confined to the pages of their journals or the walls of a school; it was alive in the hearts of every person who had ever dared to speak out, who had found strength in vulnerability, and who believed that together, even the slightest whisper could ignite a revolution of hope.

And so, as the final echoes of the night gave way to the promise of a new day, the community stepped forward with unyielding determination. They carried the memory of a quiet boy whose silence had sparked a movement and the collective strength of a generation that refused to be defined by its fears. In that new dawn, every voice would matter, every cry would be answered, and the legacy of hope, unity, and resilience would continue to resonate — forever echoing in the corridors of time.

Epilogue: The Echoes Live On

The morning air held a promise — a quiet, persistent reminder that even after the storm has passed, the echoes of what once was continue to shape the future. In the soft light of dawn, the community that had gathered over the years now stood as a living testament to the power of transformation. Every whispered cry that had sparked a revolution, every voice that had once been silenced, had found its place in a collective symphony of hope.

Tyler's memory — once a small, almost imperceptible plea in the corridors of River Valley High — had grown into a legacy that transcended time and place. It was a legacy built not on the sorrow of loss but on the resilience of a generation that refused to let silence be the end of the story. Through "The Echoes Network," through countless "Voice Circles", public art projects, and community forums, his quiet call had been transformed into a movement that would continue to inspire change for years.

In the following years, the movement evolved into something far more significant than anyone could have imagined. Evan's digital archive expanded into an interactive, multilingual platform that connected hearts across continents. Kiera's leadership, once marked by the weight of unspoken regrets, blossomed into a beacon for others, teaching the power of empathy and self-forgiveness. Born out of his need to atone for his own biases, Ben's mentorship program grew into a robust network that uplifted young voices in every corner of the community. And Melanie's vibrant, raw, and deeply personal art became a universal language, a visual memoir of transformation that spoke to every soul longing for connection.

The public events, intimate conversations, and quiet moments of reflection all converged into a single, powerful narrative: even in the most profound silence, a promise is waiting to be fulfilled. The community learned that no cry for help was ever truly lost — that every unspoken word could spark a revolution of compassion. Every gesture contributed to a tapestry of shared experiences and collective healing, from the smallest act of kindness to the grandest public celebration.

In time, the story of that quiet movement spread beyond the city's boundaries. Schools, community centers, and organizations worldwide adopted the "The Echoes Network" model, adapting it to their own cultures and needs. International forums, global summits, and collaborative art projects emerged as examples of how a single, silent plea could evolve into a worldwide call for justice and unity. Tyler's legacy, once rooted in the halls of a high school, had now become a global anthem — a reminder that every voice, no matter how quiet, has the power to change the world.

Looking back, the journey was not without its trials. There were moments of doubt and pain when the burden of responsibility threatened to overwhelm the hearts of those who led the movement. Yet, in those very moments, the seeds of resilience were sown. Every obstacle was met with a determination to rise, every setback became a lesson in empathy, and every silent cry found its echo in the hearts of those who dared to listen.

As the sun rose on a new day, the community — now a mosaic of countless voices, stories, and dreams — continued to move forward with a renewed sense of purpose. The lessons of the past were not forgotten; instead, they became the guiding light for the future. Tyler's memory lived on in every act of kindness, in every public forum where voices were raised in unison, and in every piece of art that celebrated the beauty of human connection.

In quiet moments of reflection, the founders and leaders of the movement would gather and speak softly about the past — the humble beginnings that had sparked a revolution of hope. They shared stories of early struggles, nights filled with regret, and the long, winding path that led to the realization that healing was not a destination but a continuous journey. Their conversations, filled with sorrow and joy, were a tribute to the enduring spirit of resilience and the belief that even the slightest whisper can ignite a powerful change.

Today, the legacy of that movement stands as a beacon for all who feel unheard. It is a reminder that every silent cry carries the seed of transformation within it and that by coming together, we can create a world where every voice is cherished. The echoes of the past continue to resound, not as mournful laments but as triumphant declarations of hope, unity, and the unbreakable power of connection.

As you close this book, remember that the story is not over — it is merely a chapter in the ongoing narrative of life. We have the power to listen, speak, and ignite change. May the legacy of Tyler's silent plea inspire you to believe that no voice is too small to make a difference and that every whisper of hope can one day grow into a resounding chorus for a better tomorrow.

Author's Note: The Power of Being Seen

Thank you for taking this journey with me. This book was born from a steadfast belief that even the quietest voice can trigger extraordinary change. I set out to craft a narrative that peels back the layers of personal loss and transformation while illumining the remarkable power of community and connection.

In these pages, you've met characters whose lives were reshaped by a single, almost imperceptible moment — a quiet cry that sparked a movement. Tyler's story, though fictional, stands in for every voice that has ever felt lost in the crowd, every soul that has struggled in silence. It's a reminder that our deepest challenges can catalyze profound growth and lasting impact.

Much like the turning points that define the most compelling human stories, our journey here is one of both vulnerability and relentless determination. The characters you've followed — Evan,

Kiera, Ben, and Melanie — embody that every setback can be transformed into an opportunity, and every whispered regret can ultimately become a resounding call for hope. Their experiences are not just about overcoming adversity; they're about embracing it as a stepping stone toward a future built on empathy, resilience, and shared purpose.

I aimed to tell this story with clarity and urgency — an exploration of how individual struggles can change lives when met with collective compassion. I hope this book encourages you to look around, listen closely, and discover the latent power in every silent plea. May these pages inspire you to trust in the potential of your voice and never underestimate the impact of small, courageous acts.

Thank you for reading, reflecting, and engaging with these ideas. Here's to the possibility that every whisper can become a chorus, and every quiet moment can pave the way for a brighter, more connected tomorrow. **Sumit Sharma**

Appendix:

Building Connection, Courage, and Compassion

A 25-Hour Workshop Inspired by Whispers of the Third Rail

Workshop Overview

This 25-hour workshop is designed for educators, counselors, student leaders, or youth mentors who want to foster a culture of compassion, connection, and resilience. Inspired by the themes of Whispers of the Third Rail, the exercises focus on mental health awareness, peer support, and empowering young people to advocate for themselves and others.

- Workshop Goals:
    - o Help students develop emotional awareness and

resilience

o   Build skills in listening, empathy, and leadership

o   Encourage students to create safe spaces for peers in need

o   Inspire participants to build stronger, more inclusive communities

Workshop Structure

The workshop is divided into five modules, each approximately 5hours long. Each module includes discussion prompts, group exercises, and reflection activities.

Module 1: Breaking the Silence – Creating a Culture of Trust

Focus: Identifying social isolation, learning to recognize signs of distress, and building trust through authentic conversations.

Session 1: The Power of Listening (2 Hours)

Exercise: The Quiet Circle — Participants sit in a circle. One person shares a personal challenge while others silently listen without responding. Afterward, each listener writes one encouraging note for the speaker.

Discussion Prompt: "Why do we feel pressure to 'fix' people instead of just listening?"

Session 2: Recognizing Invisible Struggles (3 Hours)

Activity: Behind the Mask — Students create two masks: one that reflects how they present themselves publicly and one that reflects what they hide.

Group Reflection: Discuss the emotional impact of pretending to be "okay" and explore ways to reach out to those silently struggling.

Module 2: Finding Your Voice — Building Courage and Advocacy

Focus: Helping students speak up for themselves and others.

Session 3: The Courage to Ask for Help (2 Hours)

Exercise: The Post-It Wall — Participants write something they're struggling with on a sticky note (anonymously). Facilitators read each note aloud, and participants brainstormed ways to offer support if they knew the writer personally.

Group Discussion: "Why is it so hard to ask for help?"

Session 4: Role-Playing Courageous Conversations (3 Hours)

Activity: Scripts for Support — Students practice scenarios where a friend is distressed. Focus on language like:

"I've noticed you've seemed off lately. Want to talk?" "I'm worried about you — how can I help?"

Group Discussion: Reflect on how these conversations felt and what made them difficult or empowering.

Module 3: Creating Safe Spaces — Building a Community of Support

Focus: Teaching students to create inclusive environments where people feel seen and valued.

Session 5: Small Acts, Big Impact (2 Hours)

Exercise: The Kindness Chain — Each participant writes a straightforward act of kindness they can commit to (e.g., "Invite someone new to sit with me at lunch"). Participants link their notes into a paper chain, symbolizing their collective commitment to creating a welcoming environment.

Discussion Prompt: "What's one small thing someone has done that made you feel seen?"

Session 6: Creating a Student Support Panel (3 Hours)

Group Activity: Students brainstorm how to start their peer-led support group like the one in Whispers of the Third Rail.

Planning Exercise: Identify key roles, meeting structures, and strategies for spreading awareness in their school or community.

Module 4: Building Resilience — Managing Stress and Emotional Health

Focus: Developing coping strategies and building emotional strength.

Session 7: Tools for Managing Stress (2 Hours)

Exercise: The Calm Jar — Each student fills a jar with small strips of paper containing affirmations, grounding exercises, or coping techniques. The jar becomes a resource for moments of anxiety or stress.

Discussion Prompt: "What helps you reset when you feel overwhelmed?"

Session 8: Practicing Gratitude and Reflection (3 Hours)

Activity: Letters of Gratitude — Each participant writes a letter to someone who positively impacted their life, expressing appreciation for their kindness.

Reflection Prompt: Encourage students to share the impact of writing (or delivering) their letter.

Module 5: Carrying the Whisper Forward — Creating a Lasting Impact

Focus: Encouraging students to take meaningful action in their communities.

Session 9: Identifying 'Invisible' Students (2 Hours)

Exercise: The Empty Chair — Participants identify groups of students who may feel overlooked (e.g., transfer students, LGBTQ+ students, students from other cultural backgrounds). They brainstorm ways to create opportunities for connection.

Discussion Prompt: "What stops people from reaching out — and how can we change that?"

Session 10: Building a Legacy of Kindness (3 Hours)

Exercise: Mural of Messages — Similar to the mural in Whispers of the Third Rail, students write words of encouragement or share a brief story about someone who impacted them. These messages can be collected into a digital space, a public art project, or a hallway display to inspire future students.

Closing Reflection: Each participant reflects on what they've learned — and writes down one way they will continue showing up for others.

Bonus Exercise: The Whisper That Saved Me

Reflection Exercise (1 Hour)

Each participant writes about a time they felt invisible — and what (or who) helped them through it.

Encourage volunteers to share their stories if comfortable.

Implementation Guide

- For Schools: Run the course over 5 weeks with two 2.5-hour sessions per week.

- For Youth Programs: Spread the content across weekend workshops or retreats.

- For Educators and Counselors: Use individual modules to supplement mental health awareness efforts.

Final Message for Participants

"We can't always see what others are carrying. But when we show up — with kindness, courage, and compassion — we remind people they aren't alone. One whisper of hope can save a life."

The WHISPER Model™

THE
WHISPER MODEL™
A Framework for Safe Conversations,
Compassion, and Courage

W – Watch for Silent Signals

H – Hold Space without Judgment

I – Initiate a Safe Conversation

S – Speak with Empathy

P – Practice Active Support

E – Encourage Professional Help

R – Reinforce Resilience and Hope

*Inspired by Whispers of the Third Rail –
Small actions, big ripples.*

The WHISPER Model™ is a structured, actionable framework designed to help individuals create safe spaces, foster meaningful connections, and provide compassionate support to those in need. Inspired by Whispers of the Third Rail, this model reflects the power of quiet actions and small moments of kindness that ripple outward to change lives.

The **WHISPER Model™** is an acronym that stands for:

W — *Watch for Silent Signals*

H — *Hold Space without Judgment*

I — *Initiate a Safe Conversation*

S — *Speak with Empathy*

P — *Practice Active Support*

E — *Encourage Professional Help*

R — *Reinforce Resilience and Hope*

Step 1: W – Watch for Silent Signals

"The loudest cries are often silent."

Key Principle: People struggling emotionally often won't ask for help directly. Learning to identify subtle signs of distress is crucial.

Silent Signals to Watch For:

- Sudden withdrawal from social groups

- Unexplained mood swings or irritability

- Decline in academic performance or work effort

- Unusual changes in eating or sleeping patterns

- Excessive self-deprecating comments

- Giving away personal belongings or acting as if they're 'saying goodbye'

Exercise: Silent Signal Spotting

Create a "Signals Board" where students anonymously describe situations when they've felt invisible. This builds awareness for spotting subtle cries for help.

Step 2: H – Hold Space Without Judgment

"People don't need you to fix them — they need you to listen."

Key Principle: Holding space means being present and allowing someone to express their emotions without interruption, judgment, or advice.

How to Hold Space Effectively:

- Use open body language (face them directly, relaxed posture)

211 THE WHISPER MODEL™

- Avoid interrupting or rushing their story

- Validate their feelings with phrases like:

  o "That sounds hard."

  o "I'm here for you."

  o "I can't imagine how you're feeling... but I'm listening."

Exercise: The 60-Second Pause

In pairs, practice sitting silently for 60 seconds after someone shares a personal story — resisting the urge to 'fill the silence.' This trains participants to embrace stillness rather than rushing to respond.

Step 3: I – Initiate a Safe Conversation

"Courage begins with a question."

Key Principle: People in distress may not know how to start the conversation — but they'll often respond if you create a safe opening.

How to Start the Conversation:

- Ask open-ended questions:

  o "Hey, I've noticed you've been quiet lately... is everything okay?"

  o "I've been thinking about you... want to talk?"

    ▪ Use non-threatening settings like walking

together, during casual activities, or sitting side-by-side.

Exercise: Conversation Role-Play

Participants pair up and practice starting conversations with someone showing signs of distress. The goal is to create safe, low-pressure dialogue.

Step 4: S – Speak with Empathy

"Empathy is louder than advice."

Key Principle: Empathy is about making the other person feel understood, not 'solving' their pain.

How to Speak with Empathy:

- Repeat key emotions you hear:
    - o "It sounds like you've been feeling overwhelmed."
- Avoid phrases that minimize feelings:
    - o "It's not that bad."
    - o "You'll get over it."
- Instead, offer supportive language:
    - o "That sounds painful... I'm here."
    - o "You're not alone in this."

Exercise: The Mirror Technique

In pairs, one person shares a challenge they're facing. The listener's goal is to repeat what they heard without adding advice or opinions.

Step 5: P – Practice Active Support

"Being there doesn't mean fixing everything — it means showing up consistently."

Key Principle: Support is an ongoing process. Simple, consistent actions often make the most significant impact.

Ways to Practice Active Support:

- Follow up regularly ("I've been thinking about you... how are you feeling?")
- Include them in activities without pressure
- Offer practical help (e.g., walking to class together, bringing them a snack, helping them stay organized)

Exercise: The Support Chain

Each participant commits to one supportive act that week and then reports back. This builds accountability and reinforces that small actions matter.

Step 6: E – Encourage Professional Help

"Caring for someone doesn't mean doing it alone."

Key Principle: While compassion matters, some situations require professional intervention.

How to Guide Someone Toward Help:

- Offer reassurance: "Getting help isn't a weakness — it's a strength."

- Provide options: "Would you like me to walk you to the counselor's office?"

- Follow up: "Did you get to talk to someone yet?"

Exercise: Help Map Activity

Students create a "Help Map" listing trusted teachers, counselors, or resources they can guide peers toward when needed.

Step 7: R — Reinforce Resilience and Hope

"Hope isn't loud — it's steady."

Key Principle: When someone feels lost or defeated, reminding them of their strengths and past victories helps rebuild their confidence.

How to Reinforce Resilience:

- Celebrate small victories: "I know how hard that must've been — I'm proud of you."

- Remind them they're not alone: "You're stronger than you think... and I'm still here."

Exercise: The Hope Letter

Each participant writes a letter to their 'future self,' reminding them of their strengths, achievements, and those who care about them. Letters are sealed and returned at the end of the course.

Implementing the WHISPER Model™

The WHISPER Model™ can be applied:

- In schools to train peer leaders
- In mental health awareness workshops
- As a guide for parents and guardians
- In youth programs, camps, and community centers

Closing Note for Participants

"Every whisper matters. Every quiet act of kindness — every word spoken with compassion — creates a ripple that can save a life. Don't underestimate the power of simply showing up. Because sometimes... one whisper is all it takes."

Copyright and Recognition

The WHISPER Model™ is an original framework designed exclusively for Whispers of the Third Rail. All rights are reserved under copyright protection.

Facilitator guides and workshop materials can be adapted for educational use, provided credit is given to the author, Sumit Sharma.

www.ingramcontent.com/pod-product-compliance
Lightning Source LLC
Chambersburg PA
CBHW070802280326
41934CB00012B/3021